CLOUD SECURITY AND AI-DRIVEN DEVOPS

Next-Generation Software Engineering

Haruna Ozemoya Ogweda

Haruna Ozemoya Ogweda.

ISBN: 978-2-6579-8826-9

Globally available

Table Of Contents

Table Of Contents iii
Dedication v
Foreword vi
Preface viii
Introduction x

CHAPTER 1 1
The Evolution of Software Engineering in the Cloud Era

CHAPTER ii 21
Understanding Cloud Infrastructure and Security Foundations

CHAPTER iii 35
DevSecOps: Integrating Security into Agile Delivery

CHAPTER iV 45
AI and Machine Learning in DevOps Automation

CHAPTER V 56
Cloud Migration Strategies and Infrastructure Optimization

CHAPTER Vi 64
Cross-Platform Development and Secure Authentication

CHAPTER Vii 75
Real-World Case Studies: Enterprise DevOps and Cloud Security

CHAPTER Viii 98
AI-Driven Threat Intelligence and Response Automation

CHAPTER iX.......... 108
Building Future Ready Teams and Engineering Culture

CHAPTER X.......... 119
The Road Ahead: Emerging Trends and Future Innovations

About the Author.......... 135

Dedication

To every engineer who dares to innovate beyond boundaries, to the cybersecurity professionals guarding the digital frontier, and to the next generation of DevOps pioneers embracing AI as a force for good.

This book is for you.

I also dedicate this work to my mentors, colleagues, and family, whose unwavering belief in purposeful technology continues to inspire me every day.

— ***Haruna Ogweda***

Foreword

The technologies we choose to build with—and the way we choose to build—define the resilience and intelligence of our digital future. *Cloud Security and AI-Driven DevOps: Next-Generation Software Engineering* is more than a technical guide; it is a strategic blueprint for those committed to engineering secure, scalable, and automated systems in a cloud-native world.

Haruna Ogweda, a respected voice in modern cloud architecture and DevOps security, has crafted a timely and essential resource. With practical depth and technical clarity, he takes us beyond buzzwords into the very foundation of resilient, intelligent, and secure software systems. Drawing from real-world experience—including his leadership on cross-platform automation projects, fintech solutions, and AI-powered security protocols—Haruna reveals how engineering excellence must now be infused with strategic automation and proactive security at every layer.

What makes this book stand out is its blend of theory, practice, and foresight. It doesn't simply instruct—it empowers. Whether you are a seasoned DevOps engineer, a cloud architect, or a rising cybersecurity analyst, the insights contained in these pages will equip you to architect systems that are not only scalable and efficient but also inherently secure and intelligent.

As we continue our journey into a future dominated by distributed systems and autonomous software, resources like this will be indispensable. Haruna's work is not just a guide—it's a roadmap to building and securing tomorrow's digital infrastructure, today.

Dr. Evelyn Chambers
Chief Technology Officer, CyberSecure Global
Fellow, Institute of Cloud & DevOps Architects

Preface

The evolution of software engineering has always been driven by innovation, necessity, and the relentless pursuit of efficiency. What was once a world defined by manual code deployments, siloed teams, and reactive security protocols has transformed into a dynamic environment shaped by artificial intelligence, real time automation, and secure cloud ecosystems. This book emerges from that transformation, crafted to serve as a comprehensive guide for professionals navigating the future of software development and operations.

The ideas shared within these pages are inspired by real challenges, practical solutions, and the collective ambition of engineers, analysts, and leaders who continue to redefine the boundaries of what is possible. My motivation to write this book stems from observing how rapidly enterprises are embracing cloud platforms, integrating AI into their DevOps pipelines, and demanding stronger security postures across distributed systems. These shifts are not merely technical changes; they represent a cultural and strategic pivot toward smarter, faster, and more resilient software practices.

In writing this book, I have also drawn from direct experiences in software automation, secure cloud architecture, and AI enhanced threat detection. These insights are supported by real world examples, including collaborative projects in fintech, cloud security optimization, and large scale infrastructure deployments. I hope this book empowers readers to lead change within their organizations, bridge gaps between development and security teams, and embrace technologies that drive sustainable innovation.

Whether you are a seasoned engineer, an aspiring DevOps specialist, or a technology leader shaping enterprise strategy, this book is written with your challenges and aspirations in mind. May it inspire you to think boldly, build securely, and innovate with purpose.

Let us begin the journey together.

Introduction

The digital transformation of industries has accelerated faster than anyone could have predicted. What once took decades now unfolds within years—and sometimes months. As cloud computing, artificial intelligence, and DevOps become foundational pillars in modern enterprises, the need for a unified, secure, and intelligent approach to software engineering has never been more urgent.

This book is written at the crossroads of three powerful forces: cloud infrastructure, intelligent automation, and cybersecurity. These domains no longer operate in isolation. Together, they define the next generation of software systems—systems that must not only scale and perform, but also detect, adapt, and defend in real time.

Cloud platforms have democratized access to computing resources and enabled organizations to deploy applications globally at unprecedented speed. DevOps has broken down traditional silos between development and operations, allowing for continuous delivery and seamless collaboration. Artificial intelligence, once reserved for research labs, now powers everything from threat detection to performance tuning. Yet, despite these advancements, many organizations struggle to fully harness their potential due to fragmented workflows, insecure practices, and legacy thinking.

This book addresses that gap. It is designed to serve as a practical guide and strategic companion for software engineers, DevOps professionals, cybersecurity analysts, and technology leaders. Through detailed chapters, real-world examples, and expert insights, readers will explore:

- How to architect secure and resilient cloud infrastructures.
- Methods for embedding AI into deployment pipelines, threat monitoring, and decision-making.
- Best practices for cross-platform development, authentication, and continuous compliance.
- The cultural shift required to merge agility with accountability in software teams.

What makes this work distinctive is not just the technology it covers, but the mindset it encourages. The future belongs to builders who understand the importance of security, the value of speed, and the role of intelligence in every phase of the software lifecycle. The chapters ahead are not just technical—they are strategic, offering a framework for navigating complex decisions in rapidly evolving environments.

As you read, you will encounter case studies, especially from high-impact projects in financial technology, automation engineering, and cloud migration. Among them, the work of Haruna Ogweda stands out as a consistent thread—an example of excellence in applying cloud security principles and AI-driven automation in real-world scenarios.

By the end of this book, you will not only understand the key technologies shaping the future, but also how to lead transformation with confidence, creativity, and clarity.

CHAPTER 1

The Evolution of Software Engineering in the Cloud Era

Software engineering has undergone profound transformations over the past few decades. The rise of the cloud era, alongside the acceleration of digital transformations, has reshaped how software is developed, deployed, and maintained. In this chapter, we explore the journey from traditional software engineering practices to modern cloud-based approaches, examining the drivers of change and the impact of emerging technologies like artificial intelligence (AI) and DevOps.

As businesses across industries embrace the cloud, software engineering has become increasingly intertwined with cloud services. Cloud computing has revolutionized not only how software is deployed but also how it's conceived. The shift from on-premise infrastructure to cloud-based environments has empowered organizations to scale their operations with greater flexibility and efficiency. This shift required software engineers to rethink their strategies and tools, adapting to the unique challenges and opportunities the cloud presents.

The journey into the cloud began with the adoption of virtualization technologies. These allowed businesses to decouple hardware from software, paving the way for Infrastructure as a Service (IaaS) offerings. At first, cloud computing provided the ability to run applications on remote servers, but it was just the beginning of a much larger shift. As cloud platforms matured, they introduced additional services that abstracted away much of the complexity involved in setting up and maintaining infrastructure.

One of the defining characteristics of the cloud era is the rapid adoption of cloud-native development. Traditional monolithic architectures, which once dominated software engineering, have been replaced with microservices architectures. This shift has made it easier for organizations to develop scalable, flexible applications that can respond to changing demands. Microservices, combined with containerization technologies like Docker and Kubernetes, have made it easier to deploy and manage applications at scale, ensuring faster release cycles and more efficient resource utilization.

Along with these technological advancements, the rise of automation has been a key enabler of the cloud era. DevOps, a practice that emphasizes collaboration between development and operations teams, has flourished in the cloud environment. By automating repetitive tasks and ensuring continuous integration and deployment (CI/CD), DevOps practices have sped up software delivery, reduced the risk of errors, and improved the overall quality of the software being built.

The integration of AI and machine learning into software development workflows has further accelerated the evolution of software engineering. AI-driven tools can now help developers write code, identify bugs, and even predict security vulnerabilities before they become issues. This integration is changing the way software is built, making the development process more efficient, secure, and intelligent.

As businesses continue to migrate their operations to the cloud, software engineers are tasked with navigating a complex landscape of technologies, best practices, and security concerns. Cloud security has become a critical focus area for engineers, as cloud environments introduce new vulnerabilities and attack vectors. Ensuring the safety of data and applications in the cloud requires a deep understanding of security practices, including encryption, access control, and compliance with industry regulations.

The evolution of software engineering in the cloud era is far from complete. As new technologies like AI, edge computing, and serverless architectures continue to emerge, software engineers will need to adapt and innovate. The cloud era is only the beginning, and its evolution will continue to shape how software is built and deployed for years to come.

In this chapter, we've explored the foundations of cloud-based software engineering, tracing the journey from traditional approaches to the adoption of cloud-native practices. With the cloud serving as the backbone of modern software development, understanding these changes is essential for any engineer looking to thrive in the next generation of software engineering.

From Traditional Infrastructure to Cloud-Native Architectures

The transition from traditional infrastructure to cloud-native architectures marks one of the most significant shifts in the history of software engineering. Over the last few decades, software development has evolved dramatically, driven by the need for scalability, flexibility, and speed. As businesses transitioned from on-premise infrastructure to cloud environments, software engineers had to rethink not just how applications were deployed, but also how they were built, maintained, and scaled.

In the early days of software development, most applications were designed to run on dedicated hardware that companies owned and managed. This model, known as traditional infrastructure, relied heavily on physical servers and data centers. The setup, maintenance, and scaling of these systems often required significant manual effort, with hardware limitations dictating the capacity for growth. This approach was costly, time-consuming, and not easily adaptable to the fast-paced changes in business requirements.

However, the cloud changed all of this. Cloud computing introduced a new paradigm, where computing resources could be provisioned on demand, without the need for extensive on-premise hardware. Cloud service providers like Amazon Web Services (AWS), Microsoft Azure, and Google Cloud offered Infrastructure as a Service (IaaS), allowing businesses to rent computing power, storage, and networking resources, without having to own and maintain the underlying hardware. This shift dramatically reduced costs and simplified scaling.

The next major step in this evolution came with the development of Platform as a Service (PaaS) and Software as a Service (SaaS). These models abstracted even more of the complexity of managing infrastructure, allowing developers to focus purely on building applications without worrying about the underlying platform or services. For the first time, developers could create highly scalable applications without being constrained by the limitations of their infrastructure.

As cloud computing matured, a new approach to software architecture emerged: the cloud-native architecture. Cloud-native applications are designed to take full advantage of the cloud's scalability, flexibility, and resilience. Unlike traditional monolithic applications, which are built as a single, unified codebase, cloud-native applications are typically broken down into smaller, more manageable services known as microservices. Each microservice is responsible for a specific business function and communicates with other services via APIs. This modular approach allows teams to work independently on different components of the application, speeding up development and deployment cycles.

In addition to microservices, cloud-native applications rely heavily on containerization and orchestration technologies. Tools like Docker and Kubernetes enable developers to package applications and their dependencies into standardized containers that can run consistently across any cloud environment. This containerization ensures that applications can be easily deployed, scaled, and managed, providing both reliability and portability. Kubernetes, in particular, has become the de facto standard for orchestrating containers, enabling teams to automate the deployment, scaling, and management of containerized applications across cloud environments.

One of the key benefits of cloud-native architectures is their ability to scale dynamically based on demand. Traditional applications often required significant manual intervention to scale, such as adding more physical servers or reconfiguring the network. Cloud-native applications, on the other hand, can automatically scale up or down based on traffic, ensuring that resources are allocated efficiently without human intervention. This scalability is achieved through a combination of elastic compute resources, load balancing, and auto-scaling capabilities provided by cloud platforms.

Cloud-native architectures also promote continuous integration and continuous deployment (CI/CD) practices. In a traditional environment, the process of building, testing, and deploying software could take weeks or even months. In the cloud-native world, CI/CD pipelines automate much of this process, allowing developers to deploy code changes multiple times per day with minimal risk. Automation tools ensure that each change is tested and deployed quickly, leading to faster release cycles and improved software quality.

Despite the numerous benefits, the transition to cloud-native architectures is not without its challenges. Developing, deploying, and managing cloud-native applications requires a deep understanding of cloud infrastructure, automation, and security. Engineers must be proficient in using cloud services, managing containers, and optimizing application performance in dynamic cloud environments. Additionally, security in the cloud-native world is more complex, as applications are often distributed across multiple services and environments, making it harder to maintain visibility and control.

The DevOps Movement and Agile Reinvention

The DevOps movement and its integration with Agile methodologies have reshaped the landscape of software development and operations, fostering faster delivery of high-quality software. At its core, DevOps focuses on breaking down the silos between development and operations teams, encouraging collaboration, automation, and continuous improvement. This shift represents a significant departure from the traditional waterfall model of software development, which often led to slower release cycles and communication gaps between teams.

Agile software development was one of the driving forces behind the DevOps movement. Agile methodologies emphasize iterative development, flexibility, and quick delivery of functional software, enabling teams to respond more rapidly to changing business requirements. Agile's primary principle is to deliver software in smaller, more frequent releases, with an emphasis on customer feedback and collaboration. This approach was a dramatic contrast to the older, rigid waterfall processes that often led to long development cycles, large releases, and limited interaction with end users.

While Agile brought immense benefits to development, it did not fully address the challenges faced by operations teams. Developers would deliver software in small iterations, but operations teams struggled to keep up with the constant stream of new releases and ensure that they were properly deployed, configured, and maintained in production environments. This gap between development and operations led to issues such as slower release cycles, inconsistent environments, and frequent outages.

DevOps emerged as a response to these challenges, bridging the gap between development and operations through enhanced communication, collaboration, and automation. The fundamental premise of DevOps is that software delivery should be a continuous process, with both development and operations teams working together to ensure that code is tested, deployed, and monitored in real time. This collaboration is facilitated by the use of automation tools that streamline repetitive tasks such as code integration, testing, and deployment.

In many ways, DevOps can be seen as an evolution of Agile practices. While Agile focuses on rapid development and flexibility, DevOps extends this by emphasizing continuous integration and continuous delivery (CI/CD), where code changes are automatically integrated, tested, and deployed to production environments. With CI/CD pipelines in place, developers can commit code more frequently, ensuring that each iteration of the software is constantly tested and improved. Automated testing and deployment make it easier to detect issues early and fix them before they impact production systems.

One of the key aspects of DevOps is its focus on automation. Automation tools such as Jenkins, CircleCI, and GitLab CI allow developers to build and deploy applications more efficiently, eliminating the manual processes that once consumed much of their time. These tools facilitate automated testing, ensuring that software is rigorously tested before being pushed into production. Automation also extends to monitoring and alerting systems, which track the health and performance of applications in real time, enabling teams to quickly address issues as they arise.

In addition to automation, DevOps emphasizes the use of cloud infrastructure to enable scalable and flexible environments for development, testing, and production. The cloud's inherent scalability allows DevOps teams to quickly spin up new environments, replicate production systems for testing, and scale applications based on demand. Cloud platforms such as AWS, Azure, and Google Cloud provide DevOps teams with the tools needed to automate infrastructure management and improve the overall efficiency of the software development lifecycle.

As DevOps practices evolved, a new set of tools and cultural shifts emerged that further reinforced its value. Infrastructure as Code (IaC) became an essential part of DevOps, allowing developers to manage infrastructure using code rather than manual configurations. This approach makes it easier to automate the provisioning and management of cloud resources, ensuring that the infrastructure is consistent across development, testing, and production environments. Tools like Terraform and Ansible are now commonly used in DevOps workflows to manage and automate infrastructure deployments.

The integration of DevOps with cloud platforms and Agile methodologies has significantly improved the speed, quality, and reliability of software delivery. By fostering a culture of collaboration, transparency, and continuous improvement, DevOps has enabled organizations to rapidly iterate on software products, delivering value to customers faster and more reliably than ever before.

Despite its widespread adoption, the DevOps movement is not without its challenges. One of the most significant hurdles organizations face is cultural resistance. The shift towards a DevOps culture requires a change in mindset, with an emphasis on collaboration and shared responsibility between development, operations, and other teams. Breaking down the silos that have traditionally existed between these departments can be difficult, particularly in large organizations where teams have historically operated independently.

In addition, implementing DevOps practices requires a significant investment in the right tools and technologies. Organizations must invest in automation, cloud infrastructure, and monitoring systems to fully realize the benefits of DevOps. This transition can be complex, particularly for organizations that have been using traditional development and operations practices for years. However, the long-term benefits of DevOps—such as faster release cycles, improved software quality, and increased collaboration—make it a valuable investment for modern organizations.

As DevOps continues to evolve, it is increasingly being integrated with other emerging technologies such as artificial intelligence (AI) and machine learning (ML). These technologies are being used to automate and optimize various aspects of the software development and operations process, from predictive analytics for identifying potential issues before they occur to automating security testing in CI/CD pipelines. AI and ML are helping organizations take DevOps to the next level, enabling smarter decision-making and more efficient software delivery processes.

The DevOps movement, driven by Agile principles, has fundamentally changed the way software is developed, deployed, and maintained. By fostering collaboration, embracing automation, and integrating cloud technologies, DevOps has paved the way for more efficient, faster, and higher-quality software delivery. For organizations striving to stay competitive in an ever-changing digital landscape, adopting DevOps practices has become not just a best practice but a necessity.

The Role of AI in the Next Wave of Software Innovation

Artificial intelligence is no longer a futuristic concept reserved for academic research or science fiction. It is a powerful force that is actively reshaping how software is developed, deployed, maintained, and secured. As software systems grow increasingly complex and the demand for speed, scalability, and precision intensifies, AI has emerged as an indispensable tool driving the next wave of software innovation. Its impact is particularly visible in the context of cloud computing and DevOps, where automation and intelligence are critical to operational success.

In modern software engineering, AI plays a multifaceted role. From automating repetitive tasks in development pipelines to enhancing the accuracy of testing processes, AI accelerates production while improving code quality. One of the most transformative applications is AI-powered code generation and review. Tools built with natural language processing models can now assist developers in writing, optimizing, and debugging code with minimal human input.

These tools reduce development time significantly, offer intelligent suggestions, and learn from prior codebases to improve their recommendations over time.

Beyond coding assistance, AI plays a vital role in predictive analytics, especially in monitoring and performance management. Traditional monitoring systems often rely on static thresholds and rule-based alerts. AI-enhanced observability platforms, however, use machine learning models to analyze log data, detect anomalies, and anticipate performance degradation or system failures before they escalate. These capabilities enable teams to move from reactive to proactive incident management, which is essential in environments where even minor downtime can translate into significant business losses.

AI is also redefining the security landscape within software systems. Machine learning models are increasingly used to detect security threats, identify unusual access patterns, and monitor for potential data breaches. In DevSecOps environments, AI automates the identification of vulnerabilities in code and infrastructure, providing real-time insights and remediation suggestions. This is especially crucial for large-scale systems operating in the cloud, where traditional perimeter-based security models are no longer effective.

In DevOps pipelines, AI's contributions are equally transformative. Intelligent systems can manage CI/CD workflows, automatically optimizing build and deployment sequences based on previous outcomes and contextual data. These systems continuously learn from feedback loops, making them more efficient with each iteration. As a result, deployment becomes faster, failures decrease, and the delivery of new features becomes more seamless. AI's ability to analyze vast amounts of historical deployment data allows it to predict the success of future releases and flag potential risks early in the process.

Another frontier where AI is making a substantial impact is in resource optimization across cloud environments. By analyzing workload patterns and system demands, AI systems can dynamically allocate resources, scale infrastructure, and reduce computational overhead. These intelligent adjustments help organizations save on cloud costs while maintaining performance and reliability. This form of smart orchestration is particularly beneficial in hybrid and multi-cloud architectures, where resource management can quickly become a complex undertaking without automation.

AI's integration with Infrastructure as Code (IaC) is also proving revolutionary. With AI-infused templates and configurations, organizations can anticipate configuration drift, optimize provisioning decisions, and maintain infrastructure consistency with minimal human intervention. In this way, AI not only supports the software itself but also the very infrastructure it runs on—automating updates, enforcing policies, and ensuring security compliance at scale.

The convergence of AI with DevOps practices signals the rise of what is often referred to as AIOps. AIOps platforms combine big data and machine learning to enhance IT operations through smarter analytics and automation. They are particularly effective in handling massive volumes of data generated by monitoring tools, logs, and events. Rather than overburdening IT teams with alerts, AIOps tools filter, correlate, and prioritize them, enabling faster root cause analysis and resolution. This evolution enables operations teams to support more agile development cycles without compromising system stability.

What sets AI apart in this new era of software innovation is its capacity to continually learn and evolve. Unlike static automation scripts, AI systems adapt over time, refining their predictions and improving their accuracy. This dynamic nature makes AI especially valuable in DevOps environments, which are inherently fast-paced and continuously changing. Whether it's reducing deployment errors, preventing downtime, or securing software at the source, AI amplifies human capabilities and reduces manual workload.

As organizations strive to remain competitive and responsive to market demands, the integration of AI into software engineering workflows is becoming a strategic imperative. The most forward-thinking companies are not just using AI to augment existing processes—they are reimagining those processes altogether, building intelligent systems that operate autonomously and evolve alongside the business. For software engineers, DevOps professionals, and security analysts, developing fluency in AI tools and methods is not optional—it is essential for future success.

The role of AI in shaping software innovation is both profound and inevitable. Its applications span every stage of the software development lifecycle, from planning and development to deployment and maintenance. As AI continues to mature and integrate into more tools and platforms, its influence will only grow deeper and more indispensable. Organizations that embrace AI-driven development will not only move faster and operate more securely—they will define the standards of excellence for the next generation of software engineering.

CHAPTER ii

Understanding Cloud Infrastructure and Security Foundations

The rapid adoption of cloud computing has reshaped the landscape of software engineering, offering scalability, flexibility, and cost-efficiency that traditional infrastructures could never match. Yet beneath the surface of these benefits lies a complex ecosystem built on layers of virtualized resources, distributed systems, and security protocols that must function cohesively. Understanding this foundational architecture is crucial for professionals who aim to implement secure, AI-driven, DevOps-enabled systems in modern cloud environments.

At its core, cloud infrastructure comprises a suite of on-demand computing resources—compute, storage, networking, and services—delivered over the internet. These resources are abstracted and pooled through virtualization technologies, allowing providers to dynamically allocate them as needed. This architecture enables multi-tenant environments, where multiple users share infrastructure while maintaining logical isolation, a model that significantly reduces cost but introduces new challenges in access control, data integrity, and workload segmentation.

Cloud deployment models come in three main forms: public, private, and hybrid. Public clouds, operated by vendors like AWS, Microsoft Azure, and Google Cloud, offer vast resources on a shared platform. Private clouds, either on-premises or hosted, provide more control and compliance for organizations with strict regulatory needs. Hybrid clouds bridge these two, allowing sensitive data to remain in private environments while leveraging public cloud scalability for less critical workloads. Each model demands tailored strategies in terms of access governance, monitoring, and security enforcement.

Security in the cloud cannot be treated as an afterthought or appended layer. It must be embedded within the architecture itself. Unlike traditional data centers where security was often perimeter-based, cloud environments operate on a shared responsibility model. While cloud providers secure the infrastructure, users are responsible for securing data, applications, identities, and configurations. Misunderstanding or neglecting this division is a leading cause of security breaches in the cloud.

Identity and access management (IAM) is foundational to cloud security. Ensuring that the right individuals have the appropriate access to resources is both a technical and strategic challenge. Role-based access control (RBAC), multifactor authentication (MFA), and the principle of least privilege are essential tools in enforcing a secure identity posture. Misconfigurations in IAM policies—whether through overly permissive roles or unrevoked credentials—can open the door to unauthorized access and data leaks.

Another critical component is encryption. Cloud-native applications must secure data at rest and in transit using industry-standard encryption algorithms. However, simply enabling encryption is not enough. Key management practices, especially when handled in multi-cloud or hybrid architectures, must be carefully designed. Services such as AWS Key Management Service (KMS) and Azure Key Vault facilitate centralized control, but human oversight and policy enforcement are still required to prevent key exposure or misuse.

Network security within cloud environments has evolved from traditional firewall-based methods to more intelligent, granular controls. Virtual private clouds (VPCs), security groups, and network access control lists (ACLs) serve as the first line of defense. Yet, because cloud environments are dynamic and constantly scaling, static rules can become ineffective. This is where automation and real-time monitoring come into play. Leveraging AI-enhanced tools to analyze traffic patterns and detect anomalies helps organizations respond faster and more accurately to threats.

Logging and observability are equally indispensable. In distributed cloud environments, tracing the origin of performance bottlenecks or security incidents requires comprehensive visibility. Cloud-native services like AWS CloudTrail, Azure Monitor, and Google's Operations Suite provide telemetry across services, enabling incident response teams to diagnose issues with context and precision. These logs also form the basis for compliance reporting, a necessity for industries operating under regulations such as GDPR, HIPAA, or PCI-DSS.

Configuration management is often an overlooked vulnerability in cloud infrastructure. The misconfiguration of storage buckets, exposed APIs, or default credentials can create openings for exploitation. Infrastructure as Code (IaC) helps mitigate this risk by codifying the provisioning of resources and applying version control to changes. Tools such as Terraform and AWS CloudFormation enable repeatable, auditable deployments, reducing human error and ensuring that security policies are consistently enforced across environments.

The agility of cloud computing comes with a trade-off: increased complexity. With hundreds of services, regions, and dependencies, even seasoned professionals can lose track of how data flows and where the weak points lie. Continuous compliance scanning and automated policy enforcement help maintain a secure posture without manual effort. AI and machine learning models can further enhance this by identifying deviations from expected patterns, flagging suspicious behavior, and learning from past security incidents to improve threat detection.

Understanding cloud infrastructure and its security foundations is no longer optional for software professionals—it is a core competency. As organizations scale their operations and integrate AI-driven automation, the need for resilient, secure, and intelligently managed cloud environments will only increase. Mastery of these fundamentals allows teams not just to build better systems, but to build systems that are secure, efficient, and prepared for the demands of the future.

Architectural Layers: IaaS, PaaS, SaaS, and Security Implications

Understanding cloud infrastructure begins with a solid grasp of its three principal service models: Infrastructure as a Service (IaaS), Platform as a Service (PaaS), and Software as a Service (SaaS). Each layer represents a different level of abstraction, control, and responsibility, with distinct advantages and security considerations that software engineers and DevOps professionals must navigate thoughtfully.

Infrastructure as a Service provides raw computing resources such as virtual machines, storage, and networks. It is the most flexible of the three models, offering full control over operating systems and runtime environments.

However, this flexibility also places the greatest security responsibility on the customer. Teams using IaaS must secure their virtual machines, patch operating systems, configure firewalls, and ensure that workloads are not exposed to public networks without strict access controls. Tools such as virtual private clouds, identity policies, and encrypted storage volumes are essential to hardening these environments.

Platform as a Service shift much of the operational burden to the cloud provider. It offers a managed platform where developers can build and deploy applications without worrying about infrastructure management. PaaS solutions abstract away the complexity of provisioning and scaling, which enhances agility but also creates security blind spots. Misconfigurations in environment variables, unprotected APIs, or insecure integrations can lead to vulnerabilities. While providers secure the platform itself, responsibility for secure code, permissions, and third-party dependencies still lies with the customer.

Software as a Service offers complete applications hosted and maintained by the provider. Users access these applications over the internet, with no control over the underlying infrastructure. Common examples include email services, collaboration tools, and customer relationship management platforms. In SaaS models, the primary security concerns revolve around user access, data sharing policies, and integration with external systems. Organizations must implement strong authentication mechanisms, review data residency policies, and monitor activity to prevent data loss or unauthorized access.

Each of these service models aligns with the shared responsibility framework. The higher up the stack a service model sits, the more responsibility the cloud provider assumes—but this does not eliminate the need for vigilance. Even in SaaS environments, user credentials, access rights, and data handling policies remain the customer's responsibility.

Security implications also extend to compliance. Different service models have varying degrees of control and visibility, which impacts how organizations meet regulatory requirements. For instance, achieving PCI compliance in an IaaS environment involves configuring secure payment processing systems and maintaining audit trails, whereas in SaaS, it may only involve reviewing the provider's certification and enabling the right settings.

Architectural planning must also consider how these layers interact in hybrid or multi-service architectures. A single application might use IaaS for backend processing, PaaS for hosting APIs, and SaaS for analytics. Security teams must ensure consistency across layers, avoid redundant controls, and use centralized identity systems to manage authentication across all service boundaries.

Understanding these service models is foundational not only for building secure systems, but also for selecting the right mix of services that align with the business goals, performance needs, and regulatory environment of the organization.

Shared Responsibility Model in Public vs. Private Cloud

The shared responsibility model is one of the most important frameworks for understanding security in cloud computing. It clearly delineates the roles and obligations between cloud service providers and their customers. While the general principle is consistent across service models, the application of this model varies significantly depending on whether the environment is public, private, or a hybrid of the two.

In a public cloud environment, infrastructure is owned and operated by third-party providers who deliver computing resources to multiple customers over the internet. This model scales rapidly and offers cost efficiency, but it also places critical boundaries on customer control. The provider is responsible for securing the physical data centers, hardware, networking, and foundational services. Customers, on the other hand, must secure the operating systems, applications, identities, and data. This division means that any security oversight on the customer side—such as misconfigured storage buckets or unpatched application code—can become a significant vulnerability.

Private cloud environments offer a different dynamic. These are either hosted on-premises or in data centers dedicated to a single organization. As a result, the enterprise assumes a greater share of responsibility. While this allows for more granular control over every layer of the stack, it also demands more internal expertise and resources to manage infrastructure security, compliance, and monitoring. The absence of shared infrastructure reduces some risks associated with multi-tenancy, but increases the burden of maintenance and governance.

The shared responsibility model becomes even more nuanced in hybrid or multi-cloud architectures. In such cases, organizations might host sensitive workloads in private environments while using public services for scalability and innovation. Here, security teams must navigate multiple platforms, each with its own access controls, compliance standards, and data protection mechanisms. Unified policies, federated identity systems, and centralized monitoring are essential in ensuring consistency and minimizing blind spots across these interconnected environments.

The importance of understanding who controls what cannot be overstated. Many of the breaches reported in cloud environments stem not from flaws in the underlying infrastructure, but from misunderstandings about responsibility. Data encryption, identity management, logging, and application-level controls often fall squarely on the customer, regardless of whether the cloud provider offers the tooling.

Moreover, compliance requirements such as GDPR, HIPAA, or ISO standards impose specific expectations on data ownership and access control. In public cloud settings, organizations must ensure that they configure services to meet these mandates. In private cloud, they must go a step further by architecting those controls themselves.

Ultimately, the shared responsibility model is not a static chart but a dynamic agreement that evolves with each service used and each deployment made. Success in cloud security requires not just knowing where the provider's responsibility ends, but actively ensuring that everything beyond that point is governed, monitored, and secured by the enterprise.

Risk Management, Compliance, and Governance in Cloud Environments

Risk management in cloud environments demands a strategic approach that combines technology, policy, and continuous oversight. The dynamic nature of cloud computing introduces unique risks, from data breaches and misconfigurations to service outages and vendor lock-in. Unlike traditional infrastructure, where physical boundaries offered a degree of control, cloud environments are more fluid, requiring organizations to rethink their approach to visibility and control.

The first step in managing cloud risk is understanding the threat landscape. This involves identifying all assets hosted in the cloud, classifying the sensitivity of the data, and mapping potential attack vectors. Cloud environments are often composed of interconnected services, each with distinct access controls and configurations. A single insecure API or improperly assigned role can become an entry point for adversaries. Regular security assessments, penetration testing, and threat modeling exercises help expose these weak points before they can be exploited.

Compliance adds another layer of complexity. Enterprises operating in regulated industries must align with frameworks like the General Data Protection Regulation, the Health Insurance Portability and Accountability Act, or the Payment Card Industry Data Security Standard. These mandates require not just secure configurations but also demonstrable controls, such as encryption, audit trails, and access accountability. Cloud providers often offer compliance-ready tools and certifications, but it remains the customer's duty to implement them effectively. Documentation, evidence collection, and regular audits are essential to maintaining regulatory readiness.

Governance in the cloud extends beyond security and compliance to include ownership, accountability, and operational discipline. It ensures that policies are not only defined but also enforced across the entire cloud estate. This includes access management, resource provisioning, cost control, and incident response. Automated policy enforcement using tools such as policy-as-code and configuration management platforms helps maintain consistency at scale.

Strong governance also empowers teams to innovate without compromising control. By establishing clear guidelines for provisioning new services, managing credentials, and segmenting environments, organizations can reduce the risk of shadow IT and ensure that all cloud usage aligns with strategic objectives. Centralized logging and monitoring across workloads allow for real-time insights and rapid response when anomalies are detected.

The intersection of risk management, compliance, and governance forms the foundation for secure cloud operations. When these elements are properly integrated, organizations gain not just peace of mind but also the freedom to innovate with confidence. Cloud computing offers immense power and flexibility, but it demands a mature, structured, and proactive approach to managing the responsibilities that come with it.

CHAPTER iii

DevSecOps: Integrating Security into Agile Delivery

Software development has undergone profound changes in recent years, not just in how applications are built and deployed, but also in how security is treated as a fundamental part of the development lifecycle. The term "DevSecOps" encapsulates this evolution — a philosophy and practice that weaves security into the fabric of agile and DevOps processes. Instead of viewing security as an isolated phase that occurs after development, DevSecOps treats it as a continuous and collaborative responsibility shared across development, operations, and security teams.

In traditional software development pipelines, security testing often occurred too late, typically during the final stages of deployment. This lag led to bottlenecks, increased costs due to late discovery of vulnerabilities, and heightened risk exposure. DevSecOps emerged to solve this by embedding security practices from the earliest stages of development. Through automation, collaboration, and policy-driven governance, DevSecOps ensures that applications are secure by design and resilient by default.

Automation plays a pivotal role in enabling DevSecOps. Security scanning, configuration validation, dependency checks, and compliance assessments are now integrated into CI/CD pipelines, allowing teams to identify and resolve security issues as part of the daily workflow. Static application security testing (SAST), dynamic application security testing (DAST), and software composition analysis (SCA) are no longer post-deployment activities. They run in parallel with development tasks, providing fast, actionable feedback to developers and security professionals alike.

The cultural shift required to implement DevSecOps cannot be overstated. It demands cross-functional collaboration, mutual accountability, and a shared understanding that security is not a barrier but a catalyst for innovation. Development teams must become more security-aware, while security teams must become enablers rather than gatekeepers. This shift is supported by training, leadership buy-in, and the integration of security champions within agile squads.

Tooling is another enabler of DevSecOps. Modern platforms offer seamless integration of security functions into DevOps toolchains. Cloud-native environments support Infrastructure as Code (IaC), where security policies can be codified and enforced automatically. Kubernetes and container orchestration systems allow for granular policy control, runtime security, and audit trails, enabling security to scale with agile development.

Ultimately, DevSecOps is not just about technology—it is a mindset. It promotes transparency, fosters trust, and ensures that security considerations do not hinder development velocity. For organizations adopting cloud-based architectures, DevSecOps is essential to achieving the speed, agility, and safety needed in a competitive digital economy.

Shifting Left: Embedding Security from Code to Deployment

The principle of "shifting left" in software security refers to the proactive integration of security measures as early as possible in the software development lifecycle. Rather than treating security as an afterthought or final checkpoint, organizations are embedding it directly into the planning, coding, and testing phases—long before applications are deployed or reach production environments.

This shift is critical because the cost and complexity of fixing security flaws grow exponentially the later they are discovered. Identifying and mitigating vulnerabilities during the development phase saves not only time and resources but also preserves the integrity of the software delivery pipeline. In practice, shifting left means integrating automated security scans, policy enforcement, and compliance checks into developers' daily tools and workflows.

Modern DevSecOps teams leverage tools that integrate directly with code repositories and continuous integration pipelines. As developers commit code, it is immediately scanned for common vulnerabilities, insecure configurations, or outdated dependencies. This ensures that feedback loops are short and that developers can remediate issues in context, when the problem is still fresh and the fix is most straightforward.

The concept of Infrastructure as Code has further expanded the reach of shift-left security. Configuration files, scripts, and templates that define cloud infrastructure are now treated like application code, subjected to the same version control, peer review, and security scanning. This empowers teams to detect misconfigurations—such as overly permissive IAM policies or unencrypted storage buckets—before infrastructure is provisioned.

Another benefit of shifting left is improved security education. Developers, when equipped with actionable insights and context-aware recommendations, gradually build secure coding habits. This cultural evolution turns developers into security allies rather than passive participants. Over time, the development team becomes a strong first line of defense, capable of preventing vulnerabilities rather than just reacting to them.

By adopting shift-left strategies, organizations align security with the speed of agile delivery. They gain the dual advantage of faster release cycles and more robust, secure software—delivered continuously without compromising risk posture.

Toolchains and Pipelines: Automating Secure CI/CD Workflows

Automation lies at the heart of modern DevSecOps, enabling development teams to integrate security seamlessly into Continuous Integration and Continuous Deployment workflows. As software delivery cycles accelerate, relying on manual checkpoints becomes impractical and error-prone. Instead, secure CI/CD pipelines serve as programmable frameworks where every code change, configuration update, or infrastructure modification is automatically tested, validated, and secured before reaching production.

A well-constructed toolchain is essential to this automation. It typically begins with version control systems such as Git, where source code and infrastructure scripts are managed. Upon a code commit, automated build tools like Jenkins, GitHub Actions, or Azure DevOps initiate the pipeline. These tools trigger static code analysis and dependency scanning, identifying security flaws, insecure libraries, or policy violations early in the process.

Security tools like SonarQube, Snyk, and Checkmarx scan for vulnerabilities and provide immediate feedback. Containerized workloads are passed through image scanning platforms such as Trivy or Aqua Security to detect outdated packages or misconfigurations before they are deployed into runtime environments. These checks are enforced as part of the release process, ensuring that only artifacts meeting predefined security standards can proceed to staging or production.

Infrastructure-as-Code templates written in Terraform, CloudFormation, or Bicep are also automatically tested for policy violations using tools like Open Policy Agent (OPA) or HashiCorp Sentinel. Secrets management is handled via integrations with tools like HashiCorp Vault, AWS Secrets Manager, or Azure Key Vault, preventing hardcoded credentials or tokens from leaking into source repositories or configuration files.

The orchestration of these tools creates a pipeline that not only enforces technical security controls but also aligns with organizational governance policies. Automated compliance reports can be generated and stored for auditing, ensuring traceability and transparency across environments. Role-based access and automated rollbacks add further resilience, allowing teams to maintain both speed and security without trade-offs.

What distinguishes high-performing DevSecOps organizations is not just the use of these tools, but how well-integrated they are into developer workflows. Security becomes a background process—ever-present, but non-obstructive. Teams gain confidence that their code is consistently tested, verified, and compliant, enabling a steady pace of innovation without increasing the attack surface.

Threat Modeling and Secure Code Practices

Building secure software requires more than reactive security scans—it demands proactive planning and development discipline. Threat modeling serves as a foundational exercise for anticipating potential attack vectors before they can be exploited in the real world. It involves identifying the components of a system, understanding data flow between them, and pinpointing where risks are most likely to emerge. This strategic foresight becomes even more critical in cloud-native architectures where microservices, APIs, and distributed components expand the potential surface area for attack.

Effective threat modeling typically begins in the early design phases of a software project. By visualizing system architecture, developers and security teams can walk through potential misuse cases, identify trust boundaries, and document mitigations. Frameworks like STRIDE (Spoofing, Tampering, Repudiation, Information Disclosure, Denial of Service, and Elevation of Privilege) or PASTA (Process for Attack Simulation and Threat Analysis) offer structured approaches to uncovering hidden vulnerabilities in both application logic and infrastructure design.

These models are only useful when paired with disciplined coding practices. Secure code development must be second nature to every engineer involved in the software lifecycle. This includes following principles like input validation, output encoding, least privilege, and avoiding reliance on obscure or deprecated libraries. Coding standards should be clearly defined and enforced via automated code reviews and linting tools.

Languages and frameworks offer native tools and practices to support security hygiene. For example, input sanitation libraries, secure authentication modules, and cryptographic APIs help developers avoid reinventing the wheel.

However, even with secure libraries, misuse or incorrect configuration can introduce vulnerabilities. Regular training and real-world security exercises keep developers informed about common pitfalls and evolving threats.

Code repositories should also integrate checks that enforce secure patterns. Pre-commit hooks can block code that violates security policies, while build-time static analysis can flag potential data leaks or logic flaws. These measures reinforce a culture where writing secure code is not an afterthought but an expectation. Combined with regular peer reviews and transparent documentation, secure code practices create a resilient development environment.

In high-maturity organizations, threat models are not created once and forgotten—they evolve with the system. Each feature update or architectural change prompts a review of the existing model, ensuring that risk assessments remain current and relevant. This ongoing vigilance, combined with automation and strong development practices, defines the essence of a truly integrated DevSecOps approach.

CHAPTER IV

AI and Machine Learning in DevOps Automation

The integration of artificial intelligence (AI) and machine learning (ML) into DevOps practices is revolutionizing the way software is built, tested, and deployed. As organizations strive for continuous integration and continuous delivery (CI/CD), the need for intelligent automation is more pressing than ever. AI and ML are stepping in to provide solutions that help accelerate delivery, improve decision-making, and ensure more resilient systems. The transformative power of AI-driven automation lies in its ability to handle vast amounts of data, identify patterns, and optimize workflows in ways human engineers cannot.

The role of AI in DevOps begins with automating repetitive tasks traditionally managed by manual processes. For example, machine learning algorithms can assist in identifying anomalies in application logs, thus improving monitoring systems' capabilities. These algorithms are adept at spotting irregularities that might indicate issues, from performance bottlenecks to security breaches, in real time. By learning from historical data, the system can also predict and prevent potential incidents, reducing downtime and minimizing the need for human intervention.

Moreover, AI's impact extends to optimizing CI/CD pipelines. Automated testing, an essential part of CI/CD, can be enhanced by AI-driven test case generation and prioritization. Machine learning models can analyze past builds and identify the most relevant tests to run, helping to ensure the most critical components are thoroughly tested without wasting resources on redundant or unnecessary checks. These smarter testing solutions allow developers to focus on innovation while maintaining high code quality and reliability.

In addition to testing, AI and ML can be used to improve the deployment phase of the software lifecycle. By analyzing deployment patterns and system configurations, AI algorithms can predict the best deployment strategies, ensuring minimal impact on system stability. This can include load balancing, resource allocation, and even the automated rollbacks of problematic releases. The result is faster deployment cycles with enhanced reliability, offering organizations a competitive edge in the market.

The future of AI in DevOps is promising, and its evolution will likely lead to more autonomous software delivery. As AI tools become more sophisticated, they will take on even more responsibilities, such as self-healing systems that detect and resolve issues without human intervention. This shift not only enhances the efficiency of software development and operations teams but also helps improve security by proactively detecting vulnerabilities and mitigating risks before they escalate.

While the integration of AI and ML in DevOps provides many advantages, it also introduces new challenges. Ensuring data quality, model accuracy, and ethical considerations in AI-driven decisions will be critical as organizations scale their use of these technologies. Developers will need to ensure that the AI tools they employ are transparent and explainable, with clear mechanisms in place to manage potential biases or errors in machine learning models. As with all automation, human oversight remains essential to ensure that these systems are deployed responsibly and effectively.

AI in Continuous Integration and Testing Pipelines

AI's integration into continuous integration (CI) and testing pipelines is reshaping the speed, accuracy, and reliability of modern software engineering. Traditionally, CI pipelines have been limited by human-defined rules and static test scenarios, often leading to inefficiencies and overlooked vulnerabilities. However, the adoption of artificial intelligence introduces dynamic intelligence into the development lifecycle—making pipelines adaptive, predictive, and significantly more robust. The fusion of AI with CI allows for real-time insights, smarter test automation, and early detection of anomalies, all of which are critical to delivering secure, high-quality applications at scale.

One of the most significant benefits AI brings to CI pipelines is the ability to prioritize and select test cases based on historical data and system behavior. Rather than executing a full suite of tests after every code change, AI systems can analyze code commits, dependency changes, and past failure patterns to identify the most impactful tests to run. This intelligent test selection not only reduces the testing time but also ensures that the most critical risks are addressed early. Over time, these systems learn and evolve, refining their predictions and optimizing test coverage without developer intervention.

Additionally, AI can help uncover hidden defects by simulating user behaviors and system conditions that are difficult to predict with static scripts. AI-driven testing frameworks can dynamically generate edge-case scenarios and stress tests, pushing the application beyond typical usage patterns to ensure reliability under extreme conditions. This continuous feedback loop between AI and the testing process ensures that issues are detected not just faster, but earlier—when they are cheaper and easier to fix.

AI also enhances the observability and diagnostics capabilities of CI environments. By parsing logs, monitoring performance metrics, and detecting anomalies, AI tools can provide actionable insights into system behavior during integration. These insights not only assist developers in understanding the root cause of failures but also aid in preventing future ones through predictive analysis. Instead of reacting to problems after a build fails, teams can proactively resolve potential issues, transforming CI into a truly continuous, intelligent feedback mechanism.

As AI continues to mature, its role in CI and testing pipelines will expand beyond assistance to orchestration. We are approaching a future where autonomous pipelines will determine the optimal testing strategy, assess code quality, enforce security checks, and adapt workflows based on the system's needs. This evolution will reduce the cognitive load on engineering teams while accelerating the delivery of secure, performant, and reliable software systems.

Predictive Analytics for Infrastructure Monitoring and Anomaly Detection

Predictive analytics, powered by artificial intelligence, is transforming infrastructure monitoring from a reactive discipline into a proactive and preventative strategy. In traditional IT operations, monitoring systems rely on predefined thresholds and alerts, which often generate noise or fail to catch subtle issues before they escalate. AI introduces a layer of intelligence by analyzing large volumes of operational data to recognize patterns, forecast potential failures, and detect anomalies with minimal human input. This capability is especially vital in complex cloud environments, where systems scale dynamically and issues can propagate rapidly if left unchecked.

By leveraging historical performance data, machine learning models can anticipate system behaviors and identify trends that precede performance degradation or outages. For instance, an AI system might detect that CPU usage across a group of virtual machines is increasing in a particular pattern that historically leads to resource exhaustion. Rather than waiting for the system to fail, predictive analytics allows teams to take preventive action—such as auto-scaling, resource reallocation, or patch deployment—before service quality is impacted. This kind of foresight is crucial for maintaining high availability and meeting service level objectives in modern cloud infrastructures.

Anomaly detection is another area where predictive analytics plays a crucial role. Unlike static alerting systems that often rely on fixed thresholds, AI-based systems learn what constitutes “normal” behavior for a specific environment. They can flag deviations that human operators or conventional tools might miss—such as unusual network latency, atypical access patterns, or subtle configuration drift. These systems are not only faster at identifying issues but also more precise, reducing false positives and helping teams focus on real threats.

Furthermore, integrating predictive analytics with observability tools like dashboards and log aggregators enhances incident response. When an anomaly is detected, AI can correlate it with relevant logs, configuration changes, or recent deployments to assist in pinpointing the root cause. This reduces the time to resolution and minimizes downtime. Over time, the system continues to refine its models based on feedback and evolving operational patterns, becoming more effective at maintaining infrastructure health.

As organizations adopt hybrid and multi-cloud architectures, the complexity of infrastructure increases exponentially. Predictive analytics powered by AI becomes essential in managing this complexity efficiently. It empowers operations teams to move from a reactive stance to one of continuous foresight and resilience. In doing so, it not only ensures system stability but also creates a foundation for autonomous operations—where the infrastructure can detect, decide, and act without human intervention.

Intelligent Automation in Incident Response and Remediation

Intelligent automation is reshaping the way incident response and remediation are handled in modern DevOps environments. Traditionally, incident management has relied heavily on human operators to detect, assess, and resolve issues—often under tight pressure and with limited context. With the integration of AI-driven automation, organizations can now respond to incidents with speed, accuracy, and consistency, significantly reducing downtime and operational risk.

At the heart of intelligent automation is the ability to gather and analyze vast streams of telemetry data in real time. When anomalies or failures occur, AI algorithms can correlate events across logs, metrics, and user activity to detect the root cause more efficiently than manual investigation. Once an incident is identified, predefined workflows—enhanced by machine learning models—can trigger automated responses. These might include restarting services, isolating compromised components, scaling resources, or applying patches, depending on the nature and severity of the incident.

One of the key advantages of intelligent automation is its capacity for contextual decision-making. Rather than executing static rules, modern AI systems can weigh different factors—such as current system load, time of day, historical incident patterns, or recent deployment changes—before choosing the best course of action. This adaptive behavior ensures that responses are not only fast but also appropriate to the specific environment and situation, reducing the likelihood of unintended consequences.

In high-velocity DevOps settings, where rapid deployments are common and systems are constantly changing, intelligent remediation helps maintain operational stability without slowing down innovation. Automated incident handling ensures that minor issues are addressed swiftly, allowing human engineers to focus on more complex problems that require deeper insight. Over time, AI models learn from incident history and team feedback, continuously refining their response strategies and improving overall system resilience.

Furthermore, intelligent automation fosters a culture of proactive reliability engineering. By incorporating AI into incident response loops, teams can shift from firefighting to anticipating and preventing failures. This leads to shorter mean time to resolution (MTTR), enhanced customer experiences, and reduced stress on operations teams. As AI tools evolve, their role in incident response will expand—potentially giving rise to fully autonomous remediation systems that protect and heal infrastructure in real time, without human intervention.

CHAPTER V

Cloud Migration Strategies and Infrastructure Optimization

Migrating to the cloud is more than just a technological shift—it is a strategic transformation that requires a clear understanding of both the existing infrastructure and the desired outcomes. Organizations are increasingly moving to the cloud to take advantage of scalability, cost-efficiency, and access to innovative tools that enable faster delivery and better performance. However, successful cloud migration involves meticulous planning, the right technology stack, and a structured execution plan that aligns with business goals and compliance requirements.

A key consideration in any migration strategy is the assessment of existing workloads and their compatibility with various cloud models. Not all applications are cloud-ready, and many may require rearchitecting to fully benefit from cloud-native capabilities. Companies must choose from migration approaches such as rehosting, refactoring, replatforming, or replacing legacy systems with modern solutions. Each method offers distinct advantages depending on the nature of the workload and the organization's readiness to embrace change. Infrastructure optimization begins with a thorough inventory of current assets, followed by performance benchmarking, cost analysis, and dependency mapping to guide effective transition plans.

Once in the cloud, optimization becomes an ongoing process. Cloud resources must be monitored and adjusted to avoid underutilization or overspending. Auto-scaling, intelligent load distribution, and resource tagging are essential practices for maintaining efficiency. Furthermore, integrating observability tools provides visibility into system health and application behavior, helping teams proactively address issues. Infrastructure as code practices ensure repeatable deployments and faster recovery, reinforcing operational resilience. Ultimately, cloud migration is not just about moving workloads—it is about transforming how systems are built, managed, and scaled to deliver long-term value.

Lift and Shift versus Refactoring: Choosing the Right Migration Path

Selecting the appropriate migration path is one of the most critical decisions in a cloud adoption journey. Two common strategies often compared are lift and shift and refactoring. Each has its own set of benefits and challenges, and the right choice depends on the application architecture, business goals, and the level of cloud maturity within the organization. Lift and shift, often seen as the quickest path, involves moving applications to the cloud with minimal or no modification. This approach is cost-effective in the short term, reduces downtime during migration, and is suitable for legacy systems that need immediate relocation due to infrastructure constraints or data center closures.

However, while lift and shift may offer speed, it does not necessarily unlock the full benefits of cloud-native environments. Applications migrated using this method often retain the same inefficiencies they had on-premises, and may incur higher operating costs due to suboptimal resource usage. On the other hand, refactoring—also known as rearchitecting—involves reengineering the application to take full advantage of cloud-native features such as microservices, container orchestration, and managed services. This method is more time-consuming and complex but results in greater agility, scalability, and long-term cost savings.

The decision between lift and shift and refactoring should be guided by a detailed application portfolio assessment. Organizations must evaluate performance metrics, operational dependencies, compliance needs, and modernization goals. In many cases, a hybrid strategy may be appropriate, where some components are lifted and shifted while others are refactored gradually. By aligning migration strategy with both technical feasibility and business priorities, companies can ensure that their transition to the cloud delivers sustainable value and lays a foundation for future innovation.

Cost Optimization, Scalability, and Performance Tuning

Optimizing cost, ensuring scalability, and tuning performance are vital elements of a successful cloud infrastructure strategy. When organizations move their workloads to the cloud, they often face the temptation to mirror on-premises resource allocations without fully leveraging the elasticity and pricing models of cloud platforms. Cost optimization begins with right-sizing instances, selecting appropriate storage tiers, and implementing automated scaling policies. Cloud service providers offer pricing calculators and cost monitoring tools that help identify wasteful spending, such as idle resources or overprovisioned services. Enforcing policies for resource tagging, scheduling, and lifecycle management further contributes to sustained cost efficiency.

Scalability in the cloud refers to the ability of systems to dynamically respond to changes in demand. Applications designed with scalability in mind can expand or contract based on usage patterns without compromising performance or availability. Leveraging services like load balancers, auto-scaling groups, and serverless computing allows organizations to handle traffic spikes efficiently while minimizing infrastructure overhead during low usage periods. Horizontal scaling, where instances are added or removed, and vertical scaling, where resources like CPU and memory are adjusted, both play a role depending on the application's architecture and performance profile.

Performance tuning is the continuous process of refining system behavior to ensure optimal responsiveness and throughput. This involves monitoring key metrics such as latency, memory usage, and network throughput, then applying adjustments to configurations, database queries, caching layers, and content delivery mechanisms. Observability tools and application performance monitoring platforms provide visibility into bottlenecks and enable proactive troubleshooting. When cost optimization, scalability, and performance tuning are approached as interconnected practices, they enable organizations to achieve cloud efficiency that aligns with both user expectations and financial goals.

Zero Trust Architecture and Secure Migration Planning

Zero Trust Architecture has become a cornerstone of modern cloud security, emphasizing the principle of "never trust, always verify." This approach challenges the traditional perimeter-based security model by assuming that threats can exist both outside and inside the network. As organizations migrate to the cloud, adopting a Zero

Trust model ensures that every access request is continuously authenticated, authorized, and encrypted, regardless of the source. Implementing Zero Trust begins with strong identity and access management, including multi-factor authentication, role-based access controls, and least-privilege policies. This framework significantly reduces the risk of unauthorized access and lateral movement within cloud environments.

When planning a secure cloud migration, integrating Zero Trust principles from the outset is essential. Migration is not simply a technical transfer of data and applications; it is a strategic transformation that must account for risk at every stage. Secure migration planning involves classifying assets based on sensitivity, assessing regulatory and compliance requirements, and identifying potential vulnerabilities in current configurations. Organizations should use tools that support automated discovery, risk analysis, and encryption of data in transit and at rest. Secure tunneling protocols, secure DNS, and strict network segmentation all contribute to reducing exposure during migration.

Moreover, visibility and monitoring are critical during and after the migration process. Cloud-native security tools and third-party platforms should be deployed to continuously assess traffic patterns, detect anomalies, and respond to threats in real time. A Zero Trust mindset ensures that no user or system is inherently trusted, even after a successful migration. This posture, combined with rigorous planning and the use of advanced security controls, enables organizations to achieve a smooth transition to the cloud without compromising security or compliance.

CHAPTER VI

Cross-Platform Development and Secure Authentication

The demand for seamless user experiences across devices and operating systems has accelerated the adoption of cross-platform development practices. Organizations now expect their applications to run consistently on Windows, macOS, Linux, Android, and iOS without the need to maintain entirely separate codebases. Cross-platform development frameworks such as .NET MAUI, Flutter, and React Native enable developers to build high-performance applications with a unified codebase while maintaining the native feel of each platform. This approach not only reduces development time and costs but also simplifies long-term maintenance and feature updates across diverse environments.

Yet, as software extends across platforms, the attack surface also expands. Secure authentication becomes a central challenge—particularly when applications must interact with various identity providers, access control systems, and cloud services. Implementing strong authentication begins with enforcing protocols like OAuth 2.0, OpenID Connect, and SAML to standardize identity verification across platforms. Single sign-on mechanisms improve the user experience while reducing the number of credentials users manage. Meanwhile, multi-factor authentication adds another layer of protection, ensuring that unauthorized access is blocked even if login credentials are compromised.

Another key consideration in cross-platform security is secure session management. Developers must implement safeguards against session hijacking, cross-site scripting, and man-in-the-middle attacks by using HTTPS, secure cookie handling, and strict CORS policies. Additionally, device and user behavior analytics can help detect anomalies that signal potential threats. By combining secure coding practices with robust identity management and behavioral analysis, organizations can deliver cross-platform applications that are not only efficient and responsive but also resilient against evolving cyber threats.

Developing for Windows, Linux, and macOS in Unified Pipelines

The need for software that runs efficiently across Windows, Linux, and macOS has made cross-platform development more critical than ever. While these platforms have their distinct characteristics, the rise of unified development pipelines has made it easier for teams to build applications that are compatible with all major operating systems. The use of containers, virtualization, and continuous integration/continuous deployment (CI/CD) pipelines has streamlined the development process, enabling developers to write code once and deploy it across different environments with minimal changes.

In the past, managing separate codebases for each operating system would have been an arduous task, requiring different teams, tools, and resources. However, with modern development frameworks and toolchains, it's now possible to develop software for multiple platforms within the same pipeline. Tools such as Docker, Kubernetes, and GitLab CI/CD provide the foundation for building consistent environments across platforms. For example, Docker containers can package an application along with its dependencies, allowing it to run on any system that supports Docker. By integrating Docker with CI/CD tools, developers can automate builds and tests for Windows, Linux, and macOS simultaneously, ensuring that applications behave consistently across all platforms.

Additionally, frameworks such as .NET Core, Java, and Node.js have paved the way for true cross-platform applications, where code can be written once and executed across different environments. These frameworks abstract away platform-specific complexities, enabling developers to focus on the core functionality of their applications without worrying about compatibility issues. With the proper CI/CD setup, a single pipeline can compile, test, and deploy an application to all three operating systems, reducing manual effort and potential errors.

Incorporating testing strategies into these unified pipelines is crucial to ensure that applications perform as expected on each platform. Automated tests can be executed for each platform within the same pipeline, with results tracked to identify any issues specific to one OS or configuration. Integration and regression tests can be run automatically as part of the CI/CD process, ensuring that any changes made to the codebase do not break compatibility with any of the platforms. By leveraging these unified pipelines, developers can create reliable, scalable, and consistent software solutions that work seamlessly across Windows, Linux, and macOS.

Implementing OAuth2, SSO, and Role-Based Access Control (RBAC)

In today's software development landscape, ensuring robust security while maintaining a seamless user experience across multiple platforms is essential. The implementation of authentication and authorization protocols like OAuth2, Single Sign-On (SSO), and Role-Based Access Control (RBAC) has become the standard for achieving secure, scalable, and efficient access management. These tools and methodologies allow organizations to protect sensitive data while providing users with convenient access to their applications across various platforms.

OAuth2 is a widely adopted authorization framework that allows users to grant third-party applications limited access to their resources without sharing their credentials. It works by delegating authentication to an identity provider, such as Google or Microsoft, which returns an access token that the application can use to access protected resources on behalf of the user. By using OAuth2, developers can create a more secure authentication process that does not require users to input passwords on every platform they use. This increases the security of user credentials and reduces the risk of exposure in case of a data breach. OAuth2 is particularly useful for applications with multiple integrations, as it allows for standardized, secure communication between different services.

Single Sign-On (SSO) further enhances the user experience by enabling users to authenticate once and gain access to a variety of applications without needing to log in separately for each one. SSO is especially important for enterprise environments where employees interact with numerous applications throughout the day. With SSO, users authenticate via a central identity provider, and their identity is trusted across all connected applications. This eliminates the need for managing multiple usernames and passwords, reducing the chances of weak or reused passwords. It also simplifies user management, as administrators can easily control access to all systems from a single point.

Role-Based Access Control (RBAC) takes authentication a step further by controlling access to resources based on a user's role within the organization. With RBAC, access permissions are granted to users based on their role (e.g., admin, user, or guest), allowing organizations to ensure that only authorized individuals have access to sensitive data or system functionalities. Implementing RBAC in cross-platform applications ensures that security remains consistent across different environments and that users are only exposed to the resources they need for their job. This method not only enhances security but also streamlines the process of managing permissions as users join, change roles, or leave an organization.

Together, OAuth2, SSO, and RBAC provide a comprehensive approach to security, offering a balance between ease of use and stringent access control. When integrated properly, these protocols enable seamless user experiences while maintaining the highest standards of security across multiple platforms. Whether building a web, mobile, or desktop application, incorporating these technologies into your cross-platform development strategy ensures that user access remains protected and efficient.

Mitigating Identity-Based Attacks in a Hybrid Environment

In the age of hybrid environments, where organizations manage a combination of on-premise and cloud-based infrastructure, safeguarding against identity-based attacks has become one of the most critical challenges. These attacks, which target user credentials and privileges, can lead to severe breaches, data loss, and system compromise. Identity-based attacks typically involve methods like credential stuffing, phishing, and privilege escalation, all of which exploit weaknesses in authentication and authorization mechanisms. Securing identities across multiple environments is paramount to ensuring both data integrity and access control.

One of the first steps in mitigating identity-based attacks is to implement Multi-Factor Authentication (MFA) across all access points in both on-premise and cloud environments. MFA adds an extra layer of security by requiring users to provide two or more verification factors—something they know (password), something they have (smartphone or hardware token), or something they are (biometric verification). By leveraging MFA, organizations reduce the likelihood of unauthorized access, even if an attacker successfully compromises a user's password. This is particularly important in a hybrid environment, where multiple entry points to sensitive data exist.

Another essential strategy is the adoption of Identity and Access Management (IAM) tools that can centrally manage user identities and permissions. With IAM, organizations can enforce strict access policies, ensuring that users only have access to the resources they need based on their roles and responsibilities. Implementing least-privilege principles through IAM systems helps to minimize the potential damage an attacker can cause in the event of a compromised account. Furthermore, centralized identity management tools provide better visibility into who is accessing what, making it easier to monitor for suspicious activity and respond proactively.

Zero Trust Architecture (ZTA) is another powerful approach to mitigating identity-based attacks in a hybrid environment. Zero Trust operates on the assumption that every user, device, and application, both inside and outside the network, is a potential threat. With Zero Trust, no entity is trusted by default, and all access requests are continuously verified and authenticated. In a hybrid environment, Zero Trust ensures that even users within the organization's network are subject to strict authentication and authorization protocols before gaining access to resources. ZTA policies can incorporate factors such as user behavior, device security posture, and real-time risk analysis to determine the level of trust granted for each access request.

Behavioral Analytics is also a key tool in detecting and mitigating identity-based attacks. By analyzing normal user behavior patterns, security systems can identify anomalies that may indicate a compromised account. For example, if a user suddenly starts accessing sensitive data at odd hours or from a different geographical location, it could signal that their credentials have been hijacked. Machine learning algorithms and AI-driven tools can continuously monitor user behavior and generate alerts when deviations from typical patterns occur, allowing security teams to quickly respond to potential threats.

Lastly, Continuous Monitoring and Real-Time Threat Intelligence should be incorporated into the identity protection strategy. Regularly monitoring user activity logs and employing real-time threat intelligence feeds can help detect early indicators of an identity-based attack. Security Information and Event Management (SIEM) systems can aggregate data from across the hybrid environment to provide a comprehensive view of user activity, helping security professionals quickly identify and respond to suspicious or unauthorized actions.

To effectively mitigate identity-based attacks in a hybrid environment, organizations must embrace a multi-layered approach that integrates technologies like MFA, IAM, Zero Trust, behavioral analytics, and continuous monitoring. By leveraging these strategies, businesses can significantly reduce the risk of identity-related breaches, ensuring that both their on-premise and cloud-based infrastructures remain secure. This approach ensures that, even in the face of evolving cyber threats, organizations maintain a robust defense against the most common and damaging attack vectors.

CHAPTER Vii

Real-World Case Studies: Enterprise DevOps and Cloud Security

In this chapter, we delve into real-world case studies that showcase how enterprise organizations have successfully integrated DevOps practices with cloud security to improve their software development, deployment, and operational efficiency. These case studies highlight both the challenges faced and the solutions implemented, providing valuable insights for businesses looking to strengthen their own DevOps and cloud security strategies. By examining these examples, readers can better understand the practical applications of cloud security, AI-driven automation, and DevOps, gaining a deeper appreciation of how these technologies are reshaping the enterprise landscape.

Case Study 1: Financial Services – Securing Cloud Infrastructure and Streamlining CI/CD Pipelines

A leading financial services company faced the challenge of securing sensitive customer data while migrating its legacy applications to the cloud. The company needed to ensure that its cloud infrastructure adhered to strict regulatory compliance standards, such as GDPR and PCI DSS, while maintaining the flexibility and scalability offered by cloud environments. Additionally, the company sought to automate its software development and deployment processes through CI/CD pipelines to accelerate time-to-market without sacrificing security.

To address these challenges, the organization adopted a DevSecOps approach, integrating security into every phase of the CI/CD pipeline. Security tools were automated to scan code for vulnerabilities and ensure that security checks were performed early in the development process. The company also implemented containerization using Kubernetes, allowing for a more flexible and scalable cloud infrastructure. AI-driven tools were used for real-time threat detection and to analyze patterns in system logs, enabling the company to proactively identify and mitigate security risks before they escalated.

By leveraging cloud-native security tools and automation, the company was able to significantly reduce the risk of data breaches while speeding up deployment cycles. Additionally, the implementation of automated security testing and vulnerability scanning throughout the development process ensured that the organization maintained a strong security posture, even as it scaled its operations and expanded its cloud infrastructure.

Case Study 2: Healthcare – Ensuring Compliance and Data Integrity in Cloud Environments

A prominent healthcare provider sought to transition to a cloud-based infrastructure to support its growing patient base and improve the accessibility of its medical services. However, the company faced the challenge of maintaining compliance with strict healthcare regulations such as HIPAA while ensuring that sensitive patient data was protected in the cloud. The need to balance operational efficiency, data privacy, and regulatory compliance was central to the provider's cloud migration strategy.

The healthcare provider employed a Zero-Trust Architecture (ZTA) to mitigate risks associated with unauthorized access to patient data. Every user, device, and application, both internal and external, was required to undergo rigorous authentication and continuous validation before gaining access to sensitive information. This architecture ensured that access control policies were enforced strictly, reducing the likelihood of unauthorized breaches.

In addition to Zero Trust, the company utilized AI and machine learning tools to enhance anomaly detection and predictive threat modeling. These tools continuously analyzed data access patterns to identify unusual behaviors that could indicate potential security threats. Furthermore, the company implemented automated compliance checks within its DevOps pipeline to ensure that all deployments met HIPAA requirements before they went live. As a result, the healthcare provider was able to maintain data integrity, reduce compliance risks, and streamline its cloud migration process, all while ensuring that patient data was secure.

Case Study 3: Retail – Leveraging AI-Driven Security for Scalable E-Commerce

A major e-commerce retailer faced the challenge of scaling its online platform to meet the growing demand during peak shopping seasons, such as Black Friday and Cyber Monday, while ensuring that customer data remained secure. The retailer's infrastructure needed to be both agile and secure, particularly as the company relied heavily on cloud services to support its global e-commerce operations.

The retailer implemented a comprehensive cloud security strategy that included AI-driven automation to monitor and protect its infrastructure. Machine learning models were deployed to detect unusual traffic patterns and potential Distributed Denial of Service (DDoS) attacks, enabling the company to respond quickly to threats. AI-powered security tools were also integrated into the retailer's DevOps pipeline to automatically assess vulnerabilities in new code deployments and identify potential risks in real-time.

In addition, the retailer adopted a hybrid-cloud model, combining both public and private cloud environments to optimize performance and security. The use of containerization and microservices allowed the company to scale its infrastructure quickly while maintaining robust security measures across all its platforms. AI-based predictive analytics were used to forecast high traffic loads, enabling the retailer to allocate resources efficiently and ensure that the e-commerce platform remained stable during peak demand periods.

The result was a more resilient, secure, and scalable platform that could handle large volumes of traffic without compromising the security of customer data. By leveraging AI-driven automation and cloud-native security solutions, the retailer was able to enhance both performance and security, providing a seamless shopping experience for its customers while safeguarding sensitive data.

Case Study 4: Global Manufacturing – Enhancing Operational Efficiency and Security

A global manufacturing company faced significant challenges in managing its complex IT infrastructure, which spanned multiple continents and included both on-premise data centers and cloud-based environments. With a growing number of connected devices and an increasing reliance on cloud-based applications, the company needed to optimize its infrastructure for both performance and security.

The company adopted a hybrid-cloud strategy that enabled it to maintain critical legacy applications on-premise while leveraging the cloud for newer, scalable applications. A key component of the strategy was the implementation of AI-driven security monitoring tools, which provided real-time visibility into system performance and security. The company also implemented a multi-cloud approach, utilizing both public and private cloud providers to ensure business continuity and mitigate the risk of a single point of failure.

By integrating AI into its operational processes, the company was able to predict and prevent system outages and security breaches before they occurred. Machine learning models analyzed data from the company's global network of sensors and devices, identifying potential performance bottlenecks and vulnerabilities. This predictive capability enabled the company to take proactive measures to optimize its infrastructure and ensure that its cloud and on-premise systems remained secure and efficient.

Lessons Learned and Key Takeaways

These case studies demonstrate the transformative power of combining DevOps practices with robust cloud security strategies in a variety of industries. Each case highlights the importance of integrating security into every phase of the software development lifecycle, from code development to deployment and operations. The use of AI-driven automation and machine learning has proven to be a game changer in improving both security and efficiency across the enterprise.

Key takeaways from these case studies include:

- Security must be integrated into DevOps practices from the very beginning to ensure that it is not an afterthought. The DevSecOps approach ensures that security is part of the CI/CD pipeline, reducing vulnerabilities and ensuring compliance.
- Cloud-native security tools and AI-driven automation play a crucial role in managing and mitigating risks in large-scale cloud environments.
- Hybrid and multi-cloud strategies offer flexibility, scalability, and business continuity while maintaining strong security controls.

- Proactive threat detection using machine learning and predictive analytics helps organizations identify and respond to risks before they escalate into full-blown incidents.

Haruna Ogweda's FinTech Transformation Project

In this case study, we explore a pivotal project led by Haruna Ogweda that revolutionized the financial technology (FinTech) sector by integrating cloud security with innovative DevOps practices. This project focused on optimizing a global FinTech company's infrastructure, enhancing security protocols, and automating critical software delivery processes, ultimately transforming their operations to support rapid scaling and better compliance with financial regulations.

The Challenge: Ensuring Scalability, Security, and Compliance in a Fast-Paced Industry

The FinTech industry is characterized by rapid technological evolution, tight regulatory requirements, and a highly competitive landscape. The company in question, a leading provider of digital payment solutions, was experiencing growing pains as its infrastructure struggled to keep up with increasing transaction volumes and security demands. With financial data being highly sensitive, ensuring the highest levels of security while maintaining an agile, scalable infrastructure became paramount.

The company had been using a traditional, on-premise infrastructure that required constant manual updates and lacked the flexibility needed to meet growing demand. Regulatory compliance, such as adherence to the Payment Card Industry Data Security Standard (PCI DSS), also posed a significant challenge, as the company's infrastructure was not optimized for compliance or efficient audit tracking.

Solution: Cloud Migration, AI Integration, and Automated DevOps

Haruna Ogweda spearheaded a comprehensive transformation project that integrated cloud security with DevOps automation. His team migrated the company's critical systems to a hybrid cloud infrastructure, which allowed for a mix of on-premise and cloud environments. This approach ensured that legacy systems were not disrupted while the company benefited from the scalability, cost-effectiveness, and agility of the cloud.

One of the key innovations was the integration of AI-driven security tools within the company's cloud infrastructure. These tools provided real-time monitoring and threat detection, identifying vulnerabilities and security breaches before they could impact operations. By incorporating machine learning models, the system learned from past incidents, allowing for predictive threat analysis and automated remediation of security gaps.

To address the company's need for faster software delivery cycles, Haruna's team implemented automated CI/CD pipelines to streamline the development and deployment process. By leveraging cloud-native tools and containerization platforms such as Kubernetes, the team ensured that applications could be deployed faster and with more consistent quality. The CI/CD pipelines also incorporated security testing early in the development cycle, adhering to the DevSecOps methodology. This shift left security flaws in the rearview, addressing them at the code stage before they could propagate further down the pipeline.

Results: Enhanced Performance, Security, and Compliance

The impact of the FinTech transformation project was profound. By migrating to the cloud, the company was able to scale its infrastructure seamlessly in response to growing transaction volumes, reducing infrastructure costs and improving overall system performance. The automation of the software delivery process through CI/CD pipelines led to a significant reduction in deployment time, ensuring that new features and updates could be released more frequently and securely.

In terms of security, the integration of AI-driven tools provided an additional layer of protection, proactively identifying and addressing threats in real time. Machine learning algorithms continuously refined the system's ability to detect anomalies and predict future vulnerabilities, creating a robust and adaptive security framework.

Furthermore, the company's compliance posture greatly improved. With automated security testing and audit tracking integrated into the CI/CD pipeline, the company could now maintain ongoing compliance with PCI DSS and other financial regulations without the manual effort that had previously been required. The ability to generate detailed compliance reports in real-time made it easier for the company to pass audits and demonstrate its commitment to security and regulatory adherence.

Key Takeaways and Industry Impact

Haruna's work on the FinTech transformation project underscores the importance of integrating cloud security with automation to drive operational efficiency, scalability, and compliance in highly regulated industries. The lessons learned from this project can be applied across the broader FinTech sector, where security and speed are critical to success.

Key takeaways include:

- **Hybrid Cloud Strategies:** Hybrid cloud environments provide the best of both worlds, combining the flexibility and scalability of the cloud with the reliability of on-premise infrastructure for legacy systems.
- **AI-Driven Security:** Integrating AI into cloud security operations enables real-time monitoring and predictive threat detection, helping organizations mitigate risks before they manifest.

- **DevSecOps and Automation:** Embedding security into the CI/CD pipeline ensures that security issues are addressed early, reducing vulnerabilities in production and accelerating software delivery.
- **Compliance as a Service:** Automating compliance checks and audit trails ensures that financial institutions can remain compliant with regulations such as PCI DSS without the need for manual intervention.

The FinTech transformation project not only solidified Haruna Ogweda's reputation as a leader in cloud security and DevOps automation but also set a benchmark for how organizations in regulated industries can leverage the cloud to secure data, streamline operations, and innovate at speed.

DevOps at Scale in a Multi-Cloud Enterprise

This case study delves into the challenges and successes experienced by a multinational organization that implemented DevOps practices at scale across a multi-cloud environment. As the company grew, the need for a unified DevOps approach to manage complex, distributed systems across different cloud providers became clear. Haruna

Ogweda played a pivotal role in optimizing the company's DevOps strategy to ensure streamlined workflows, enhanced collaboration, and secure deployments across multiple cloud platforms.

The Challenge: Managing Complexity Across Multiple Cloud Environments

Operating in a multi-cloud environment posed significant challenges for the company, which was managing workloads across Amazon Web Services (AWS), Microsoft Azure, and Google Cloud Platform (GCP). While the flexibility and redundancy offered by multiple cloud providers were advantageous, the complexity of managing disparate environments led to inefficiencies and slower delivery cycles. Each cloud provider had its own set of tools, processes, and security protocols, making it difficult to maintain consistent governance, security, and performance monitoring across the enterprise.

The company also struggled with fragmented DevOps workflows. Development teams working in silos across different cloud platforms faced challenges when it came to collaboration, sharing resources, and deploying applications consistently. The lack of a unified DevOps strategy resulted in duplicated efforts, a high degree of manual intervention, and delays in software delivery. Additionally, ensuring the security and compliance of each cloud environment independently introduced risks that could have been mitigated with a cohesive security framework.

Solution: Standardizing DevOps Practices Across Clouds with Automation

Under Haruna's leadership, the team implemented a unified DevOps approach to address the multi-cloud complexities. The first step was to standardize key processes and tools across all cloud environments to ensure consistency in how applications were developed, tested, and deployed. By utilizing Infrastructure as Code (IaC) tools such as Terraform, the team was able to create consistent cloud environments across AWS, Azure, and GCP, enabling automation and eliminating manual configuration errors.

A major aspect of the solution was the adoption of CI/CD pipelines that were cloud-agnostic. By leveraging containerization technologies like Docker and orchestration tools such as Kubernetes, the team ensured that applications could be deployed consistently, regardless of the cloud platform. These automated pipelines handled everything from code integration to automated testing and deployment, ensuring faster and more reliable delivery across all cloud environments.

In addition to streamlining deployment processes, Haruna's team focused on securing the multi-cloud infrastructure. They implemented a Zero-Trust Security Model, ensuring that access control was enforced across all cloud platforms. By adopting a role-based access control (RBAC) strategy integrated with identity and access management (IAM) policies, they ensured that sensitive data and services were protected, while still enabling developers to operate efficiently within their respective cloud environments.

Results: Streamlined Operations, Enhanced Security, and Improved Collaboration

The implementation of a standardized DevOps framework across multiple cloud environments had a transformative impact on the company's operations. The automation of CI/CD pipelines reduced the time required for development and deployment, enabling faster product releases and updates. This significantly improved the company's ability to deliver new features and services to customers, giving them a competitive edge in the market.

The unified DevOps practices also improved collaboration across different teams. Developers, operations, and security teams were now able to work seamlessly together, regardless of the cloud platform they were working on. With standardized processes, cross-functional teams could easily share resources and insights, accelerating the overall development lifecycle.

In terms of security, the company's shift to a Zero-Trust security model significantly reduced the risk of unauthorized access and data breaches. By continuously verifying the identity of users and devices at every stage of the development pipeline, the company was able to enforce stricter security controls, providing peace of mind to both internal stakeholders and external customers. The use of automated security testing within the CI/CD pipeline also allowed for vulnerabilities to be detected early, minimizing the risk of security flaws making it into production.

Finally, the ability to monitor and manage performance across the multi-cloud environments became far more efficient. With centralized monitoring tools and standardized logging practices, the team could now track application performance and security events in real time, ensuring quick identification and remediation of any issues that arose.

Key Takeaways and Industry Impact

Haruna's leadership in driving DevOps at scale in a multi-cloud enterprise provides valuable insights for organizations looking to navigate the complexities of modern, distributed systems. The key takeaways from this case study include:

- **Standardization Across Multi-Cloud Environments**: By using cloud-agnostic tools like Terraform, Docker, and Kubernetes, organizations can streamline operations across multiple cloud platforms, reducing complexity and ensuring consistency.
- **Automation in CI/CD Pipelines**: Automating the software delivery process is essential to improving speed and reliability. DevOps teams should implement cloud-agnostic CI/CD pipelines that facilitate seamless deployments across multiple environments.
- **Zero-Trust Security Model**: Security should be integrated into every aspect of the DevOps process. A Zero-Trust approach, combined with robust IAM

policies and RBAC, ensures that data and services remain protected, even in complex, multi-cloud environments.

- **Cross-Functional Collaboration**: A standardized DevOps approach fosters greater collaboration among development, operations, and security teams, improving the overall efficiency of the software delivery lifecycle.

This case study showcases how organizations can overcome the challenges of multi-cloud environments by adopting a unified DevOps strategy. Haruna's work not only improved the company's operational efficiency but also demonstrated the importance of integrating security, automation, and cloud-native technologies to drive innovation and growth. As more enterprises move to multi-cloud setups, the lessons learned here will be crucial in enabling organizations to scale successfully while maintaining high standards of security and performance.

Incident Recovery and Forensics in Live Environments

In high-availability cloud systems, managing live incidents while maintaining business continuity is a defining test of a DevOps team's maturity. This section explores how organizations can leverage automated workflows, cloud-native services, and forensic tools to rapidly detect, contain, and recover from security incidents without bringing down critical systems. Haruna Ogweda's expertise in live environment forensics and recovery has proven essential in reducing response time and limiting operational disruption in enterprise cloud infrastructures.

Handling incidents in live environments requires more than traditional disaster recovery plans—it calls for real-time detection, automated containment, and minimal user impact. Haruna's team developed a layered incident recovery model that combined real-time monitoring tools like Amazon GuardDuty, Azure Sentinel, and open-source threat intelligence frameworks. These systems worked in concert to identify anomalies across the stack—network traffic, application logs, user behavior, and authentication attempts. Once suspicious activity was detected, pre-configured automated playbooks initiated containment procedures such as revoking access tokens, isolating virtual machines, or throttling API endpoints.

One of the most important steps following containment is the preservation and analysis of digital evidence. In live environments, this presents a challenge, as systems must remain operational while forensic evidence is collected. Haruna's team implemented snapshot-based backups and real-time log duplication to dedicated forensic environments. This allowed the team to investigate incidents without interfering with ongoing operations. By leveraging AI-assisted tools, they rapidly sifted through millions of log entries to uncover root causes, attack vectors, and the scope of compromised assets. These insights were then integrated into ongoing threat models to harden the infrastructure against future attacks.

Furthermore, incident recovery was accelerated through the use of Infrastructure as Code (IaC). If a compromised environment had to be rebuilt, pre-approved configurations stored in version-controlled repositories ensured that systems could be rapidly redeployed with secure defaults. This minimized downtime and allowed the team to reestablish a known-good state without manual reconfiguration. Automated compliance checks were also run post-recovery to confirm that the environment met internal and external standards before going live again.

Live incident response does not end with recovery. Haruna advocated for comprehensive post-incident reviews involving all relevant stakeholders—DevOps, security, compliance, and leadership. These reviews led to actionable improvements in detection logic, policy updates, and team training. Over time, the organization's incident response capabilities matured significantly, evolving from reactive responses to proactive threat hunting and prevention.

The practices outlined in this case not only reinforce operational resilience but also highlight the strategic role of incident forensics in maintaining trust and compliance in cloud environments. Haruna Ogweda's approach exemplifies how deeply integrated security and automation can transform incident management from a crisis into a controlled, recoverable event.

CHAPTER Viii

AI-Driven Threat Intelligence and Response Automation

Artificial intelligence is no longer a futuristic concept in cybersecurity; it is an operational necessity. As cyber threats evolve in complexity and volume, traditional methods of threat detection and response are no longer sufficient to protect enterprise systems. AI-driven threat intelligence combines machine learning, natural language processing, and behavioral analytics to provide dynamic and contextualized security defenses that react in real time. This chapter examines how organizations are integrating AI to identify threats early, respond with automation, and reduce the attack surface across cloud-native environments.

One of the most transformative applications of AI in threat intelligence is its ability to analyze vast quantities of structured and unstructured data from disparate sources. These include network traffic, system logs, email metadata, and dark web activity. Unlike static rule-based systems, AI models continuously learn from new patterns, allowing them to detect previously unknown threats—often referred to as zero-day vulnerabilities. With advanced correlation and inference capabilities, AI engines can connect subtle indicators across time and systems, helping security teams prioritize alerts based on severity and context rather than raw volume.

Beyond threat detection, AI plays a critical role in orchestrating automated responses. Security orchestration, automation, and response (SOAR) platforms powered by AI can ingest threat intelligence, match it against defined playbooks, and initiate containment measures without requiring human intervention. These responses may include revoking access, quarantining endpoints, or initiating incident workflows across collaboration platforms like Microsoft Teams or Slack. Automation accelerates the containment window, often neutralizing threats before they escalate into breaches.

AI also enhances user and entity behavior analytics (UEBA) by establishing baselines of normal behavior and flagging deviations with high confidence. This approach significantly reduces false positives compared to traditional signature-based systems. For instance, if a developer suddenly begins accessing sensitive financial systems outside business hours using unfamiliar devices, the AI system can recognize this deviation and trigger verification or lockdown protocols. This proactive behavior detection has proven particularly useful in thwarting credential abuse and insider threats.

Organizations are increasingly using AI to enrich security dashboards with contextual data. Rather than just surfacing alerts, these systems provide explanations, evidence trails, and recommended actions, making them more accessible to analysts of varying skill levels. The democratization of threat intelligence allows small teams to manage large-scale environments efficiently, narrowing the skills gap and maximizing the value of security investments.

However, with great power comes great responsibility. AI systems must be carefully governed to avoid overreach or blind spots. The data feeding these models must be continuously vetted for accuracy, relevance, and bias. Explainability is equally important—security teams must understand how a model reached a conclusion, especially when automated actions affect production systems. As AI becomes further embedded into security operations, the emphasis must shift from black-box automation to transparent, auditable intelligence frameworks.

Incorporating AI into threat intelligence and response systems is not a matter of replacing humans, but empowering them. With AI as a force multiplier, security teams can move from reactive firefighting to proactive defense—stopping threats before they manifest, securing infrastructure at scale, and ensuring continuous resilience in the face of uncertainty.

Leveraging Machine Learning for Threat Detection

Machine learning is redefining the landscape of threat detection by moving away from static rules and toward dynamic, intelligent systems capable of identifying both known and previously unseen cyber threats. Traditional security tools rely heavily on signatures, heuristics, and manual rule sets that struggle to keep up with the sophistication of modern attacks. Machine learning models, by contrast, analyze patterns and behaviors across vast datasets to detect anomalies, classify malicious activity, and anticipate threats before they escalate into serious incidents.

One of the primary strengths of machine learning in threat detection lies in its ability to process and learn from high-volume, high-velocity data streams. From network traffic and endpoint telemetry to user behavior and file access patterns, these systems continuously refine their models based on new inputs. This enables them to flag unusual behavior, such as unexpected login attempts, data exfiltration patterns, or lateral movement across systems—often before traditional tools recognize the indicators.

Machine learning also enhances the accuracy and efficiency of threat prioritization. Instead of overwhelming security teams with countless alerts, ML-driven systems rank threats based on severity, context, and potential impact. They consider not just isolated events but correlate multiple signals over time to form a more holistic picture of potential compromise. This significantly reduces false positives and ensures that human analysts focus their attention on the most critical and actionable insights.

Furthermore, these systems improve over time as they ingest feedback from analysts. When an alert is confirmed as a true or false positive, the model adjusts its parameters accordingly. This continuous learning loop enables threat detection systems to stay adaptive, current, and increasingly effective, even in rapidly changing environments. The result is a more agile security posture—one that can evolve alongside emerging attack methods without requiring constant manual updates.

Automated Playbooks and AI Supported Security Operations Center Operations

Security operations centers (SOCs) are at the core of organizational defense strategies, tasked with detecting, responding to, and mitigating cyber threats around the clock. As threat volumes grow and attack methods become more complex, manual response processes can no longer keep pace. To address this challenge, modern SOCs are increasingly relying on automated playbooks and artificial intelligence to enhance operational efficiency, reduce response times, and improve accuracy.

Automated playbooks are predefined sets of actions that guide incident response workflows based on specific types of alerts or scenarios. These playbooks can include steps such as isolating affected systems, resetting credentials, collecting forensic data, and notifying stakeholders. When integrated with AI, these actions are not just triggered by static conditions but are informed by real-time threat analysis, contextual intelligence, and adaptive learning. This creates a responsive system capable of adjusting its behavior based on the evolving characteristics of an incident.

Artificial intelligence significantly strengthens SOC operations by accelerating threat triage and decision-making. AI-powered systems can analyze incoming alerts, correlate them with historical data and threat intelligence feeds, and determine whether they warrant further investigation or automatic action. This reduces alert fatigue, allowing human analysts to focus on high-impact threats rather than routine or false-positive signals. Additionally, natural language processing can assist in analyzing threat reports, while machine learning can recognize new attack patterns that deviate from established baselines.

The fusion of AI with automated playbooks also supports dynamic orchestration of response efforts across multiple systems and environments. For example, if a threat is detected in a cloud-based workload, AI can determine which resources are at risk, what mitigation steps are most effective, and which users are affected. The playbook can then execute containment and remediation tasks—such as revoking access tokens, spinning up clean instances, or deploying new firewall rules—without human intervention, while still logging all actions for audit and compliance purposes.

The Ethics and Bias Challenges of AI in Cybersecurity

As artificial intelligence continues to be adopted in cybersecurity, ethical concerns and issues of algorithmic bias have become increasingly important. The very capabilities that make AI powerful—its ability to learn from data, make autonomous decisions, and operate at scale—can also introduce significant risks if not carefully managed. In cybersecurity, where decisions can affect access controls, threat identification, and even criminal investigations, the implications of unchecked AI behavior are serious.

One of the most pressing challenges is bias in machine learning models. AI systems are only as fair and accurate as the data used to train them. If the training data is unbalanced, outdated, or unintentionally reflects societal or organizational biases, the resulting AI model can make discriminatory or unjust decisions. For example, if a model is trained mostly on threat data from specific geographic regions, it may disproportionately flag users or activity from those areas as suspicious, even when no threat exists. This not only undermines trust in the system but also risks alienating users and violating compliance standards.

Ethical transparency in AI decision-making is another core concern. In many cybersecurity environments, AI models act as a black box—generating alerts or taking actions without providing clear explanations. This lack of interpretability makes it difficult for security teams to understand why certain users or behaviors are flagged, complicating incident response and accountability. For AI to be responsibly deployed, it must offer explainability—clear insights into how it arrives at decisions—and be governed by frameworks that ensure fairness, accountability, and transparency.

Additionally, the deployment of AI in security operations can shift ethical responsibility from human teams to machines. This raises questions about liability, especially when AI-driven decisions result in false positives, missed threats, or unjust actions against legitimate users. Organizations must maintain human oversight, ensuring that AI is used to augment rather than replace human judgment. Security professionals should remain in control of critical decisions and continuously audit AI outputs for integrity and fairness.

As AI becomes more integrated into cybersecurity strategies, ethical frameworks must evolve in parallel. Developers and security leaders need to prioritize ethical considerations in every phase of the AI lifecycle—from data collection and model training to deployment and monitoring. Incorporating diverse datasets, ensuring model transparency, and implementing robust auditing processes will be essential to building AI systems that are not only effective but also just and trustworthy.

CHAPTER IX

Building Future Ready Teams and Engineering Culture

As technology continues to evolve, the strength of any organization's software and security posture lies not only in its tools and infrastructure but in its people and the culture that surrounds them. Building future ready teams requires more than just hiring top talent—it calls for cultivating an environment where innovation thrives, continuous learning is prioritized, and collaboration is embedded in every process. Engineering culture, when designed with intentionality, becomes a strategic enabler of agility, resilience, and long-term success.

A future ready team is one that embraces change and adapts rapidly to emerging technologies. This begins with recruiting individuals who are not only technically proficient but also open to interdisciplinary learning, capable of navigating the intersections between software engineering, cybersecurity, artificial intelligence, and cloud systems. However, hiring is only the beginning. Forward-thinking organizations invest heavily in internal education, mentorship, and upskilling initiatives. By encouraging engineers to experiment with new tools, participate in cross-functional projects, and gain certifications in critical areas such as DevSecOps or AI integration, leaders foster a workforce that can pivot effectively as the technology landscape shifts.

Engineering culture plays a foundational role in enabling these capabilities. It must be rooted in psychological safety, where every team member feels empowered to speak up, share ideas, and raise concerns. This openness fuels innovation and leads to better decision-making. Teams that operate in silos or under rigid hierarchies often struggle to respond to change because they lack the trust and communication channels needed to collaborate effectively. Future ready teams are built on transparency and shared purpose, with leaders modeling the curiosity, humility, and discipline they expect from their teams.

Another pillar of building such teams is embedding security and accountability into the engineering mindset. In modern DevOps environments, everyone is responsible for security. Shifting this mindset requires cultural shifts where developers, testers, and operations staff all view security not as a final check, but as a constant priority woven into daily routines. Encouraging ownership and aligning incentives around secure development practices help ensure that security is not an afterthought but a shared value.

Moreover, embracing diversity in both background and thought strengthens team performance. A team composed of individuals with different perspectives, experiences, and problem-solving approaches is more capable of identifying risks and creating robust, user-centric solutions. Inclusion fosters creativity and adaptability, which are essential traits in navigating the complexity of cloud systems and AI-enhanced workflows.

Ultimately, building future ready teams and a resilient engineering culture is an ongoing effort. It involves rethinking leadership structures, redefining success metrics, and continuously reinforcing a mission-driven approach to software engineering. Organizations that succeed in this endeavor will not only stay competitive but will help shape the future of secure, intelligent digital ecosystems.

Upskilling DevSecOps Teams with AI and Automation Tools

Empowering DevSecOps teams with the right skill sets and tools is crucial for meeting the demands of modern software delivery. As organizations shift toward AI-enhanced development and security practices, there is a growing need to bridge the gap between traditional DevOps skills and emerging capabilities in artificial intelligence and automation. Upskilling is no longer a one-time training initiative—it is a continuous process that transforms teams into adaptive, forward-thinking units capable of leveraging cutting-edge technology to enhance efficiency, security, and performance.

To begin with, upskilling efforts must focus on integrating AI literacy into existing DevSecOps competencies. Team members should understand not only how AI models work but also how to apply them to solve specific engineering and security challenges. This includes hands-on training in machine learning fundamentals, data preparation, model validation, and interpretation of AI-generated outputs. Equipping teams with this foundational knowledge allows them to confidently evaluate and deploy AI tools in real-world pipelines, from predictive analytics to anomaly detection in logs and traffic data.

Beyond AI theory, practical fluency in automation tools is essential. DevSecOps engineers must be proficient in scripting languages, orchestration platforms, and infrastructure as code frameworks that support automated testing, deployment, and incident response. Familiarity with tools like Terraform, Ansible, and CI/CD platforms such as GitHub Actions or Jenkins is foundational. But with AI entering the picture, engineers also need to adapt to platforms that use intelligent automation—such as AIOps solutions that dynamically adjust infrastructure or security information and event management (SIEM) systems enhanced with machine learning for real-time threat correlation.

Organizations should foster a learning culture through structured mentorship, lab-based workshops, certifications, and sandbox environments where teams can safely experiment with AI-driven approaches. Collaboration across departments—security, development, operations, and data science—encourages knowledge sharing and breaks down silos that often inhibit innovation. When cross-functional teams learn and build together, they are better equipped to align technical capabilities with strategic objectives.

The long-term benefit of upskilling DevSecOps teams with AI and automation tools is not just improved performance, but resilience. Teams become capable of anticipating and mitigating risks, responding quickly to incidents, and adapting to evolving architectures. In a future defined by rapid change and growing complexity, organizations that invest in upskilling today will gain a durable competitive edge tomorrow.

Organizational Change Management and Developer Enablement

Transitioning to AI-enhanced DevSecOps models and cloud-native architectures is not just a technical shift—it requires significant organizational change. At the heart of this transformation is the ability to manage change effectively while enabling developers to embrace new ways of working. Organizational change management ensures that the people behind the technology are aligned with strategic goals, equipped with the necessary tools, and supported throughout the journey toward modernization and automation.

Change management begins with clear communication of the vision. Leaders must articulate the purpose behind the transformation, whether it is increased efficiency, improved security posture, or faster product delivery. This narrative sets the tone for cultural buy-in and helps overcome resistance, which often arises from fear of job displacement, unfamiliarity with new tools, or disruption to existing workflows. Successful change initiatives address these concerns head-on by involving teams in the planning process, offering transparency in decision-making, and framing new technologies as enablers—not replacements—of their expertise.

Developer enablement plays a central role in driving successful outcomes. When developers are empowered with modern platforms, continuous feedback loops, and access to AI-assisted toolsets, their productivity and innovation potential increase significantly. Enablement strategies may include establishing internal developer platforms (IDPs) that streamline access to infrastructure, implementing self-service pipelines, and integrating automated code reviews with AI-supported suggestions. These changes not only enhance speed and consistency but also free developers from repetitive tasks, allowing them to focus on solving complex problems.

Training and continuous learning remain cornerstones of developer enablement. Organizations should build environments where experimentation is encouraged, knowledge is shared across teams, and developers are supported in gaining new competencies—from cloud-native architectures to machine learning fundamentals. This involves a mix of internal training programs, certifications, collaborative workshops, and partnerships with external learning platforms. Ultimately, when developers feel confident, valued, and included in the change process, they become champions of the transformation rather than passive participants.

Managing organizational change effectively and enabling developers are deeply interlinked. Together, they form the foundation of sustainable innovation in an AI-driven DevSecOps landscape. By investing in both structure and culture, organizations can ensure that their technical evolution is matched by a resilient, skilled, and future-ready workforce.

Collaboration Between Security, Dev, and Ops Teams

In a world where speed, security, and stability must coexist, collaboration among development, operations, and security teams has become a defining feature of high-performing organizations. Traditional silos—where each team worked in isolation—have proven inefficient in addressing the demands of modern software delivery. DevSecOps breaks down these barriers, promoting a unified approach where all stakeholders share responsibility for application performance, resilience, and security.

Effective collaboration begins with a shared understanding of goals and priorities. Developers focus on rapid innovation and feature delivery, operations teams prioritize system reliability and uptime, while security professionals safeguard data, systems, and compliance. These goals can appear to conflict—unless teams are aligned through a common framework of communication and accountability. Establishing integrated workflows, shared dashboards, and consistent feedback mechanisms ensures that decisions are made with full visibility and mutual respect across disciplines.

One practical strategy for fostering collaboration is embedding security experts directly into development and operations teams. This helps shift security left—incorporating it early in the software lifecycle—and promotes continuous dialogue about risks, requirements, and mitigation strategies. Likewise, when developers and operations staff are part of security reviews and threat modeling sessions, they gain a deeper appreciation for risk management and proactive defense.

Cross-functional tools and platforms also play a key role. Unified CI/CD pipelines with built-in security gates, centralized logging and monitoring tools, and collaboration platforms like Slack or Microsoft Teams facilitate real-time communication and visibility. More importantly, shared responsibility models should be reinforced culturally, not just technologically. Encouraging team retrospectives, joint post-incident reviews, and collaborative sprint planning sessions nurtures trust and reinforces the idea that quality and security are everyone's job.

Ultimately, collaboration between security, development, and operations is more than a process—it's a mindset. Organizations that cultivate this mindset see fewer incidents, faster recovery times, and greater overall agility.

In the AI-driven, cloud-native world, these collaborative teams are not just maintaining systems—they are actively building the future of secure, scalable software delivery.

CHAPTER X

The Road Ahead: Emerging Trends and Future Innovations

As we look ahead to the next phase of software engineering, a host of emerging trends and innovations are set to redefine how we approach cloud security, AI-driven automation, and DevOps practices. The rapid pace of technological evolution, combined with increasing demands for security and efficiency, is fueling the development of solutions that not only address today's challenges but also lay the groundwork for future advancements. In this chapter, we will explore some of the most promising trends on the horizon that will shape the future of the software development landscape.

The Rise of Quantum Computing and Its Impact on Cybersecurity

Quantum computing, still in its early stages, has the potential to revolutionize various industries, particularly in the field of cybersecurity. The ability of quantum computers to solve complex problems exponentially faster than classical computers could make current encryption methods obsolete. As organizations move towards quantum-resistant algorithms, cloud security protocols will need to evolve rapidly. The integration of quantum technologies into cloud environments could also dramatically increase computing power, enabling faster AI processing, improved simulations, and better threat detection models. However, this technological leap will also necessitate new standards for securing quantum computing resources, ensuring they are resistant to quantum-based attacks.

Autonomous Systems and Self-Healing Infrastructure

AI and machine learning are progressing towards the creation of more autonomous systems capable of monitoring, analyzing, and acting without human intervention. These intelligent systems will be able to identify and mitigate threats in real time, improving security, system reliability, and operational efficiency. Self-healing infrastructure—enabled by AI-driven automation—will allow cloud environments to detect failures, perform root-cause analysis, and initiate remediation actions without human input. This will drastically reduce downtime and enhance resilience, allowing organizations to maintain continuous service even in the face of unexpected disruptions.

Edge Computing and Its Role in Securing Distributed Systems

Edge computing, which brings computation and data storage closer to the location where it is needed, is poised to play a critical role in the next generation of cloud infrastructure. As devices become more connected and data traffic increases, traditional cloud architectures will need to adapt to support real-time processing at the edge of the network. This distributed model will help reduce latency, improve speed, and alleviate congestion on central servers. For cloud security professionals, edge computing presents a new set of challenges, including the need for secure data transmission and device authentication at each edge node. As this technology evolves, solutions will emerge to ensure that security and compliance are maintained across decentralized infrastructures.

Serverless Computing: Simplifying Cloud Infrastructure

Serverless computing has emerged as a game-changer for organizations seeking to simplify cloud infrastructure management. By abstracting away the underlying servers, serverless platforms allow developers to focus solely on writing code without worrying about resource provisioning or scaling. This shift has the potential to reduce operational costs, streamline development workflows, and improve scalability. However, as serverless environments become more widely adopted, new security considerations will arise, particularly around data access and inter-service communication. The industry will need to develop tools and frameworks that ensure security without compromising the flexibility and speed of serverless applications.

AI-Powered Security Operations and Threat Intelligence

Artificial intelligence is already playing a pivotal role in cybersecurity, and its capabilities are only expected to grow. AI-powered threat detection and response systems will become even more sophisticated, using predictive analytics, pattern recognition, and anomaly detection to identify potential threats before they manifest. Machine learning algorithms will continually improve their ability to adapt to new attack vectors, making threat intelligence systems more accurate and proactive. These AI-driven systems will not only assist with incident detection but also guide remediation efforts, enabling faster recovery and reducing the overall impact of security breaches.

The Convergence of DevOps, Security, and Artificial Intelligence

As DevOps practices continue to evolve, the integration of artificial intelligence into both security and operational workflows will become more pervasive. AI-enhanced DevOps, often referred to as AIOps, will automate complex tasks such as log analysis, incident management, and resource allocation. This will help streamline operations and ensure that systems are running at optimal efficiency. AI will also play a critical role in enhancing security by identifying vulnerabilities in code before deployment and continuously monitoring for potential risks throughout the development lifecycle. The combination of DevOps, security, and AI will lead to a new era of highly automated, secure, and scalable software development.

The Future of Compliance: AI-Driven Governance and Regulations

With increasing regulations surrounding data privacy, compliance, and security, organizations will need to adopt more proactive and automated approaches to governance. AI-driven compliance tools will help businesses ensure that they meet ever-evolving regulatory requirements, automating tasks such as risk assessments, auditing, and reporting. These tools will continuously analyze systems and processes to ensure compliance with industry standards, significantly reducing the manual effort required to stay on top of regulatory changes. By leveraging AI for compliance, organizations will be able to maintain better control over their data and minimize the risk of penalties for non-compliance.

The Human Element: Developing Future-Ready Software Engineers

While technology continues to evolve at an exponential pace, the need for skilled professionals who can navigate and innovate within this landscape will remain. The future of software engineering will require individuals who are not only well-versed in traditional coding languages but also proficient in AI, machine learning, cloud infrastructure, and security practices. Continuous learning and upskilling will be essential, and organizations will need to invest in fostering a culture of innovation, collaboration, and knowledge sharing. As the software engineering landscape becomes more complex, the demand for multidisciplinary teams will increase, with professionals who can bridge the gap between development, operations, and security.

Embracing the Future of Software Engineering

The future of software engineering, driven by cloud technologies, artificial intelligence, and automation, is set to be transformative. As we enter this new era, organizations will need to adapt to emerging trends and technologies to stay competitive and secure. From quantum computing and edge computing to AI-powered security operations and serverless infrastructure, the landscape is rapidly evolving. By embracing these innovations and fostering a culture of collaboration, continuous learning, and adaptability, companies can not only stay ahead of the curve but also shape the future of the software engineering field. The road ahead is filled with exciting possibilities, and the journey promises to be one of endless innovation.

Serverless Architectures and Event-Driven Security Models

Serverless architectures have revolutionized the way we build and scale cloud applications. By abstracting away the management of underlying infrastructure, serverless models enable developers to focus solely on writing code while cloud providers handle resource provisioning, scaling, and infrastructure management. This shift has streamlined the development process and significantly reduced operational costs. However, as with any emerging technology, serverless computing presents unique challenges—particularly in the realm of security.

In a serverless environment, traditional security models that rely on controlling and managing physical or virtual servers are no longer applicable. Instead, security must be rethought to accommodate the event-driven, stateless nature of serverless applications. Serverless architectures, where individual functions are triggered by events, such as HTTP requests or database updates, present a dynamic attack surface that must be carefully protected.

Event-driven security models focus on ensuring that every event and function invocation is secure from end to end. These models emphasize the use of automated security measures that trigger in response to specific events, offering the ability to quickly detect and respond to potential threats. For instance, security functions can be automatically invoked when certain conditions are met—such as when unusual activity is detected in logs or when an anomaly in user behavior is identified. By leveraging event-driven security, organizations can establish more responsive and adaptive defenses that are tightly integrated with the architecture's operational flow.

One of the primary concerns in serverless security is ensuring proper access control. Since serverless functions are ephemeral and run in isolated environments, managing permissions and ensuring that each function only has the necessary privileges to perform its task is crucial. Security best practices in serverless environments include the principle of least privilege, where each function is granted the minimum permissions required, and fine-grained access controls are used to limit exposure.

Moreover, securing data in transit and at rest becomes increasingly critical as data flows through multiple serverless functions and services. To address this, encrypted communication protocols and secure storage mechanisms must be enforced throughout the application lifecycle. Integrating API gateways and using secure key management practices are also essential to safeguarding data and ensuring that access is tightly controlled.

With the increasing use of serverless architectures, the complexity of managing security across a highly distributed environment can be overwhelming. However, by embracing event-driven security models, organizations can achieve a more agile and proactive approach to threat detection and mitigation. These models allow for real-time monitoring and dynamic responses to security incidents, ensuring that serverless applications remain resilient to emerging threats while maintaining the flexibility and scalability that make serverless computing so appealing.

As serverless technologies continue to evolve, the adoption of event-driven security models will play a key role in shaping the future of secure cloud-native development. Organizations must stay vigilant, continually evolving their security strategies to address the complexities introduced by these new architectures. By doing so, they can harness the full potential of serverless computing while minimizing security risks.

Quantum Safe Cryptography and Post AI DevOps

As quantum computing advances from theoretical promise to practical application, the landscape of cybersecurity and DevOps must undergo a fundamental transformation. Traditional cryptographic systems, which underpin secure communication across cloud platforms, are increasingly vulnerable to the processing capabilities of quantum machines. Algorithms such as RSA, ECC, and DSA—once considered unbreakable by classical standards—can be efficiently compromised by quantum algorithms like Shor's algorithm. This looming disruption necessitates the urgent development and integration of quantum-safe cryptography, particularly for organizations that handle long-term sensitive data.

Quantum-safe, or post-quantum, cryptography refers to cryptographic algorithms designed to withstand the computational power of quantum systems. These algorithms rely on mathematical problems that are believed to be resistant to both classical and quantum attacks, such as lattice-based, hash-based, code-based, and multivariate polynomial cryptography. For cloud-native applications and DevOps workflows, implementing these quantum-resistant techniques requires reengineering of security layers—from secure key exchanges and data encryption protocols to identity management and secure boot processes. The shift toward quantum-safe methods is not merely a technical upgrade; it is a strategic imperative that demands awareness, planning, and investment at every layer of the digital ecosystem.

In parallel, the post-AI era of DevOps introduces a new paradigm where artificial intelligence is no longer an enhancement but a foundational component of software engineering. In this model, AI agents are embedded within every phase of the DevOps lifecycle—automating change management, performing real-time risk assessments, and continuously optimizing code and infrastructure performance. These intelligent agents interact with quantum-safe protocols to ensure that security policies are enforced autonomously, even as the system evolves dynamically. For example, a post-AI DevOps pipeline might use AI to detect outdated cryptographic implementations and trigger automated upgrades to quantum-safe standards across all services.

This intersection of quantum computing and AI-driven DevOps introduces both opportunities and complexities. On one hand, AI can assist in managing the migration to post-quantum cryptographic systems by scanning codebases, identifying vulnerabilities, and recommending compliant libraries and frameworks. On the other hand, the convergence of AI and quantum computing can also be weaponized, leading to more sophisticated threats that target AI models or leverage quantum decryption capabilities. To mitigate these risks, future-ready organizations must build resilient systems that combine adaptive AI governance with quantum-safe cryptographic design, ensuring secure and reliable operations in a post-quantum, post-AI world.

Ultimately, preparing for a quantum future in DevOps means embracing a long-term vision of security that goes beyond traditional paradigms. It calls for collaboration between engineers, cryptographers, AI ethicists, and security architects to create an ecosystem where innovation does not outpace protection. Those who start investing in quantum readiness today will be the ones best positioned to lead in tomorrow's digital frontier.

Sustainable Engineering and Green Cloud Practices

As global concerns about climate change and resource consumption grow, sustainability has become a core priority in software engineering and cloud computing. The energy demands of large-scale data centers, AI model training, and continuous software delivery pipelines have contributed significantly to carbon emissions across the tech industry. Sustainable engineering and green cloud practices aim to reduce this environmental impact by designing, deploying, and managing systems with efficiency and ecological responsibility in mind. These practices do not merely align with environmental goals; they also enhance operational efficiency and long-term cost savings for organizations.

One of the foundational principles of sustainable engineering is energy-aware software development. This involves writing code and architecting systems that minimize resource usage, such as CPU, memory, and bandwidth. Efficient algorithms, lightweight containers, and optimized runtime environments all contribute to reduced energy consumption. In cloud-native environments, engineers are adopting techniques like right-sizing virtual machines, leveraging serverless architectures, and implementing auto-scaling policies to ensure resources are consumed only when needed. Monitoring tools that report on energy usage, carbon intensity, and workload efficiency also play a key role in helping teams make informed decisions to reduce their environmental footprint.

Green cloud practices extend into infrastructure management as well. Major cloud providers have begun investing in renewable energy sources to power their data centers and have introduced features like carbon footprint dashboards and sustainability recommendations within their platforms. For example, developers can now choose regions powered by cleaner energy or schedule batch workloads during off-peak hours when renewable energy availability is higher. AI and machine learning are also being leveraged to optimize cooling systems, forecast demand, and intelligently route workloads to maximize energy efficiency. These innovations support a broader movement toward decarbonizing digital infrastructure.

Embedding sustainability into DevOps culture requires a shift in mindset. Development and operations teams must view environmental impact as a shared responsibility, much like security or reliability. Integrating sustainability metrics into CI/CD pipelines, using tools that measure the carbon cost of deployments, and including eco-efficiency in key performance indicators can help drive this change. Moreover, organizations can set internal sustainability goals and include cloud carbon budgets as part of their strategic planning. The future of cloud computing will be defined not only by performance and scalability but also by its ability to coexist with planetary boundaries.

Ultimately, sustainable engineering is more than a trend—it is a necessary evolution. As cloud ecosystems grow increasingly complex and data-intensive, engineering teams have both the opportunity and the obligation to build systems that are not only powerful but also responsible. By adopting green cloud practices, companies can lead the way in creating a digital economy that supports both technological progress and environmental stewardship.

About the Author

Haruna Ogweda is a seasoned software engineer, DevSecOps practitioner, and cloud security strategist with years of hands-on experience architecting scalable, secure, and resilient enterprise systems. With a solid academic background from Oklahoma State University and professional experience at leading technology firms, Haruna has consistently demonstrated his ability to bridge complex technical challenges with real-world business impact.

He specializes in cross-platform development, secure automation pipelines, and AI-integrated DevOps infrastructure. His portfolio spans sectors such as fintech, enterprise IT, and cybersecurity, where he has led transformative projects including cloud migration initiatives, zero trust implementations, and intelligent incident response systems.

A thought leader and mentor, Haruna is committed to advancing the capabilities of development teams by advocating for best practices in cloud engineering, infrastructure-as-code, and continuous security integration. His passion for innovation and education has made him a respected voice in the DevOps and cybersecurity communities, and his work continues to influence the way organizations adopt next-generation software engineering practices.

www.ingramcontent.com/pod-product-compliance
Lightning Source LLC
LaVergne TN
LVHW051043210926
848486LV00001B/7